The Truths
We Hold

The Truths We Hold

An American Journey

Kamala Harris

Adapted for young readers
by Ruby Shamir

PENGUIN BOOKS

PENGUIN BOOKS

An imprint of Penguin Random House LLC, New York

First published in the United States of America by Philomel Books,
an imprint of Penguin Random House LLC, 2019
Published by Penguin Books, an imprint of Penguin Random House LLC, 2020
This work is based on *The Truths We Hold: An American Journey*, by Kamala Harris,
copyright © 2019 by Kamala D. Harris, published by Penguin Press,
an imprint of Penguin Random House LLC

Visit us online at penguinrandomhouse.com

Library of Congress Cataloging-in-Publication data is available.

Printed in the United States of America

Penguin Books ISBN 9780593113172

1 3 5 7 9 10 8 6 4 2

Edited by Jill Santopolo.
Design by Jennifer Chung.
Text set in Adobe Garamond Pro.

The publisher does not have any control over and does not assume any
responsibility for author or third-party websites or their content.

To my darling husband:
Thank you for always being patient,
loving, supportive, and calm.
And most of all, for your sense of "the funny."

Contents

PREFACE

Most mornings, my husband, Doug, wakes up before me and reads the news in bed. If I hear him making noises—a sigh, a groan, a gasp—I know what kind of day it's going to be.

November 8, 2016, had started well—the last day of my campaign to be a U.S. senator from California. I spent the day meeting as many more voters as I could, and of course voting with Doug at a neighborhood school up the street from our house. We were feeling pretty good. We had rented a huge place for my Election Night party, with a balloon drop waiting to go. But first I was going out for dinner with family and close friends—a tradition dating back to my first campaign nearly a decade and a half earlier. People had flown in from all across the country, even overseas, to be with us—my aunts and cousins, my in-laws, my sister's in-laws, and more, all gathered for what we hoped would be a very special night.

I was staring out the car window, reflecting on how far

we'd come, when I heard one of Doug's signature groans.

"You gotta look at this," he said, handing me his phone. Early results for the presidential election were coming in. Something was happening—something bad. By the time we arrived at the restaurant, the gap between the two candidates had shrunk a lot, and I was inwardly groaning as well. I was starting to worry that it was going to be a long, dark night while we waited to find out who was going to be our next president.

We settled in for a meal in a small room off the main restaurant. Emotions were running high, but not for the reasons we had thought they would be. On the one hand, while polls hadn't yet closed in California, we were optimistic that I was going to win. Yet even as we prepared for that hard-earned celebration, all eyes were on our screens as state after state came back with numbers that told a troubling story for the race for president.

At a certain point, my nine-year-old godson, Alexander, came up to me with big tears welling in his eyes. I assumed one of the other kids in our group had been teasing him about something.

"Come here, little man. What's wrong?"

Alexander looked up and locked eyes with me. His voice

was trembling. "Auntie Kamala, that man can't win. He's not going to win, is he?" Alexander's worry broke my heart. I didn't want anyone making a child feel that way. Eight years earlier, many of us had cried tears of joy when Barack Obama was elected president. And now, to see Alexander's fear . . .

His father, Reggie, and I took him outside to try to console him. "Alexander, you know how sometimes superheroes are facing a big challenge because a villain is coming for them? What do they do when that happens?"

"They fight back," he whimpered.

"That's right. And they fight back with emotion, because all the best superheroes have big emotions just like you. But they always fight back, right? So that's what we're going to do."

Shortly after, we learned I had won my race. We were still at the restaurant.

I was overcome with gratitude, both for the people in that room and the people I had lost along the way, especially my mother, who had died seven years before. I tried to savor the moment, and I did, if briefly. But, like everyone else, I soon turned my eyes back to the television.

After dinner, we headed to our Election Night party, where more than a thousand people had gathered to celebrate. I was no longer a candidate for office. I was a U.S. senator-elect—the first black woman from my state, and the second in the nation's history, to earn that job. I had been elected to represent more than thirty-nine million people—roughly one out of every eight Americans from all backgrounds. It was—and is—a humbling and extraordinary honor.

My team clapped and cheered as I joined them in the small room behind the stage. It all still felt overwhelming. My staff formed a circle around me as I thanked them for everything they'd done. We were a family, too, and we had been through an incredible journey together. But now, almost two years after the start of our campaign, we had a new mountain to take.

I had written a speech based on the assumption that Hillary Clinton would become our first woman president. But that was not to be. As I looked out at the room many people were in a state of shock as they watched the outcome of the presidential race unfold.

I told the crowd we had a task in front of us. I said the stakes were high. We had to be committed to bringing our country together to protect our American values and ideals. I thought of Alexander and all the children when I posed a question:

"Do we retreat or do we fight? I say we fight. And I intend to fight!"

I went home that night with my extended family, many of whom were staying with us.

No one really knew what to say or do. Each of us was trying to cope in our own way. I changed into sweatpants and joined Doug on the couch. I then proceeded to eat an entire family-size bag of classic Doritos. Didn't share a single chip.

But I did know this: one campaign was over, but another challenge was about to begin. One that called on us all to join. This time, it was a battle for the soul of our nation.

In the years since, we've seen a White House that has lived down to the fears that had panicked Alexander on Election Night.

But we are better than this. Americans know we're better than this. And we're going to have to prove it. We're going to have to fight for it. On July 4, 1992, one of my heroes and inspirations, former Supreme Court Justice Thurgood Marshall, gave a speech that deeply resonates today. "We cannot play ostrich," he said. "Democracy just cannot flourish amid fear. Liberty cannot bloom amid hate. Justice cannot take root amid rage. America must get to work. . . . We must dissent from the indifference. We must dissent from the apathy. We must dissent from the fear, the hatred, and the mistrust."

This book grows out of that call to action, and out of my

belief that our fight must begin and end with speaking truth.

We cannot solve our most stubborn problems unless we are honest about what they are, unless we are willing to have difficult conversations and accept what facts make plain.

We need to speak truth: that there are forces of hate in this country—racism, sexism, homophobia, transphobia, and anti-Semitism—and we need to confront them. We need to speak truth: that, with the exception of Native Americans, we all descend from people who weren't born on our shores—whether our ancestors came to America willingly, with hopes of a prosperous future, or forcibly, on a slave ship, or desperately, to escape a painful past.

We need to speak truth about what it will take for all American workers to earn a living with dignity and decency. We must speak truth about who we send to jail in this country and why. We must speak truth about companies that make a profit taking advantage of the most vulnerable among us. And I intend to do just that.

Just two more things to mention before we get started:

First, my name is pronounced "comma-la," like the punctuation mark. It means "lotus flower," which is an important symbol in Indian culture. My mom was from India and she wanted to give me a name that celebrated her family's background. A lotus grows underwater, its flower rising above the surface while its roots are planted firmly in the river bottom.

And second, I want you to know how personal this book is for me. This is the story of my family. It is the story of my childhood. It is the story of the life I have built since then. You'll meet my family and my friends, my colleagues and my team. I hope you will cherish them as I do and, through my telling, see that nothing I have ever accomplished could have been done on my own.

—Kamala, 2018

One

FOR THE PEOPLE

I still remember the awe I felt the first time I walked into the Alameda County Superior Courthouse, in Oakland, California, as an employee.

It was 1988, and I was an intern during my last summer of law school. I had a sense that I wanted to work in the district attorney's office after I got my degree, but having never seen the job up close, I hadn't made up my mind.

The sun shone brightly on the courthouse. The building stood apart on Lake Merritt, taller and more regal than other buildings nearby. Though from certain angles, it looked like a wedding cake. In its own way it was grand, and I felt my heart race as I climbed up the stairs to the main entrance.

I was the first to arrive at the orientation session. Within a few minutes, the rest of my fellow clerks showed up. There was only one woman among them, Amy Resner. As soon as the session was over, I asked her for her phone number. In that male-dominated environment, it was refreshing to have at least one female colleague. She remains one of my closest friends today, and I'm godmother to her children.

As summer interns, we had very little power or influence. Our job was to watch and learn, and help out where we could. It was a chance to get a taste of how the criminal justice system worked from the inside, what it looked like when justice was served—and when it wasn't. We were placed with attorneys, seasoned prosecutors, who were bringing all kinds of cases to trial, and we had the chance to be in the room—and part of the process—of putting together a case.

I'll never forget the time my supervisor was working on a case involving a drug bust. The police had arrested a number of people who had illegal drugs, but also an innocent woman; she had been at the wrong place at the wrong time and had been swept up, too. I hadn't seen her. I didn't know who she was or what she looked like. I didn't have any connection to her, except for the report I was reviewing. But there was something about her that caught my attention.

It was late on a Friday afternoon, and most people had gone home for the weekend. In all likelihood, a judge wouldn't see her until Monday. That meant she'd have to spend the weekend in jail.

Then I started thinking: *Does she work weekends? Is she going to have to explain to her boss where she was? Is she going to get fired?*

Even more important, I knew she had young children at home, so my thoughts turned to: *Do they know she's in jail? They must think she did something wrong. Who's taking care of them right now? Is there even someone who can? What if the Child Protective Services agency gets called because no one is watching her kids. My God, her children could get taken away from her!*

Everything was on the line for this woman: her family, her job, her standing in her community, her dignity, her freedom. And yet she'd done nothing wrong.

I rushed to the clerk of the court and begged to have the judge return for just five minutes, so we could get her released. All I could think about was her family and her frightened children. Finally, as the minutes in the day wound down, the judge returned. I watched and listened as he reviewed her case, waiting for him to give the order. Then, with the pound of a gavel, just like that, she was free. She'd get to go home to her children in time for dinner. I never did get the chance to meet her, but I'll never forget her.

It was a defining moment in my life. It became crystal clear to me how, even on the edges of the criminal justice system, the stakes were so high and intensely human. Even with the limited power of an intern, people who cared could do justice. It proved to me how much it mattered to have compassionate people working in the district attorney's office. Years before I would be elected to run a major prosecutor's office, this was one of the victories that mattered the most. I knew she was going home.

And I knew the kind of work I wanted to do, and who I wanted to serve.

The courthouse wasn't far from where I grew up. I was born in Oakland, California, in 1964 and spent the early years of my childhood living on the boundary between Oakland and Berkeley.

My father, Donald Harris, was born in Jamaica in 1938. He was a brilliant student who immigrated to the United States after being admitted to the University of California at Berkeley. He went there to study economics and would go on to teach economics at Stanford University, where he still works.

My mother, Shyamala Gopalan, began her life thousands of miles to the east, in southern India. She was the oldest of four children—three girls and a boy. Like my father, she was a gifted student, and when she showed a passion for science, her parents encouraged and supported her.

She graduated from the University of Delhi at nineteen. And she didn't stop there. She applied to a graduate program at Berkeley, a university she'd never seen, in a country she'd never visited. It's hard for me to imagine how difficult it must have been for her parents to let her go. Commercial jet travel was only just starting to spread globally. It wouldn't be a simple matter to stay in touch—there were no personal computers, no cell phones, no email. Yet, when my mother asked permission to move to California, my grandparents didn't stand in the way. She was a teenager when she left home for Berkeley in 1958 to pursue a doctorate degree and was on her way to becoming a breast cancer researcher.

My mother was expected to return to India after she completed her degree. Her parents had an arranged marriage—they hadn't chosen to marry each other; their parents had made the decision for them. It was assumed my mother would follow a similar path. But fate had other plans. She and my father met and fell in love at Berkeley while participating in the civil rights movement, the decades-long struggle for justice and equal rights no matter the color of one's skin. Her marriage—and her decision to stay in the United States—was the ultimate act of her independence and of love. My parents had two daughters together. My mother received her PhD at age twenty-five, the same year I was born. My beloved sister, Maya, came two years later. Family lore has it that, in both pregnancies, my mother kept working right up to the moment of delivery—one time, she went into labor while she was at the lab, and the other while she was making apple strudel. (In both cases, knowing my mom, she would have insisted on finishing up before she went to the hospital.)

Those early days were happy and carefree. I loved the outdoors, and I remember that when I was a little girl, my father wanted me to run free. He would turn to my mother and say, "Just let her run, Shyamala." And then he'd turn to me and say, "Run, Kamala. As fast as you can. Run!" I would take off, the wind in my face, with the feeling that I could do anything. (It's no wonder I also have many memories of my mother putting Band-Aids on my scraped knees.)

Music filled our home, and every night, I would fall asleep to the sounds of jazz recordings that my dad spun on our record player or my mom singing along to the gospel music she loved. But the harmony between my parents didn't last. In time, things got harder. They stopped being kind to each other. I knew they loved each other very much, but they just couldn't get along. By the time I was five years old, the bond between them had given way. They separated shortly after my dad took a job at the University of Wisconsin, and they divorced a few years later. They didn't fight about money. The only thing they fought about was who got the books.

It was hard on both of them. I think, for my mother, the divorce represented a kind of failure she had never considered. Her marriage was as much an act of rebellion as an act of love. After all, she had challenged the tradition of arranged marriages, which had been hard enough to explain to her parents. Explaining the divorce, I imagine, was even harder. I doubt they ever said to her, "I told you so," but I think those words echoed in her mind regardless.

Maya was still a toddler at the time of their separation, a little too young to understand what was going on, to feel the hardness of it all. I have often felt a pang of guilt because of something Maya never got to experience: I knew our parents when they were happy together. Maya never really did.

My father remained a part of our lives. We would see him on weekends and spend summers with him. But it was really my mother who took charge of our upbringing. She was the one most responsible for shaping us into the women we would become.

And she was extraordinary. My mother was barely five foot one, but I felt like she was a giant. She was smart and tough and fierce and protective. She was generous, loyal, and funny. She had only two goals in life: to raise her two daughters and to end breast cancer. She pushed us hard and with high expectations as she nurtured us. And all the while, she made Maya and me feel special, like we could do anything we wanted to if we put in the work.

My mother had been raised in a household where political activism and civic leadership came naturally. Her mother, my grandmother, Rajam Gopalan, had never attended high school, but she was a skilled community organizer. She would take in women who were being abused by their husbands, and then she'd call the husbands and tell them they'd better shape up or she would take care of them. She used to gather village women together, teaching them about their health and how they could prevent unplanned pregnancies. My grandfather P. V. Gopalan had been part of the movement to win India's independence. From them, my mother learned that it was service to others that gave life purpose and meaning. And from my mother, Maya and I learned the same.

My mother inherited my grandmother's strength and courage. People who knew them knew not to mess with either. And from both of my grandparents, my mother developed a strong political awareness. She was conscious of history, conscious of struggle, conscious of inequities. She was born with a sense of justice imprinted on her soul. My parents often brought me in a stroller with them to civil rights marches. I have young memories of a sea of legs moving about, of the energy and shouts and chants. Social justice was a central part of family discussions. My mother would laugh telling a story she loved about the time when I was fussing as a toddler. "What do you want?" she asked, trying to soothe me. "Fweedom!" I yelled back, echoing a call-and-response I'd heard at a protest.

My mother surrounded herself with close friends who were really more like sisters. My godmother, "Aunt Mary," a fellow Berkeley student, was one of them. My mother and Aunt Mary met through the civil rights movement that was taking shape in the early 1960s. As black students spoke out against injustice, a group of passionate, keenly intelligent, politically engaged young men and women found one another—my mother and Aunt Mary among them.

They went to peaceful protests where they were attacked by police with hoses. They marched against the Vietnam War and for civil rights and voting rights. They went together to see Dr. Martin Luther King Jr. speak at Berkeley, and my mother had a chance to meet him. She told me that at one anti-war protest, the marchers were confronted by the Hell's Angels motorcycle gang. She told me that at another, she and her friends were forced to run for safety with me in a stroller, after violence broke out against the protesters.

But my parents and their friends were more than just protesters. They were big thinkers, pushing big ideas, organizing their community. Aunt Mary, her brother (my "Uncle Freddy"), my mother and father, and about a dozen other students organized a study group to read the black writers that the university was ignoring. They received prominent guests, too, including civil rights and intellectual leaders like LeRoi Jones and Fannie Lou Hamer. My uncle Aubrey taught San Francisco State University's first-ever class in black studies.

These were my mother's people. In a country where she had no family, they were her family—and she was theirs. From almost the moment she arrived from India, she chose and was welcomed to and enveloped in the black community. It was the foundation of her new American life.

We were also close with my mother's mentor, Howard, a brilliant endocrinologist who took her under his wing. When I was a girl, he gave me a pearl necklace that he'd brought back from a trip to Japan. (Pearls have been one of my favorite forms of jewelry ever since!) Aunt Lenore was one of my mother's closest confidantes and she showed me the beauty of the outdoors as we chased fireflies in the fading light of the day together. On the nights we'd go to Aunt Mary's house, Uncle Sherman and I played chess together. He loved to explain the bigger implications of the game: the idea of being strategic, of having a plan, of thinking things through multiple steps ahead, of predicting your opponent's actions and adjusting yours to outmaneuver them. Every once in a while, he would let me win.

I was also very close to my mother's brother, Balu, and her two sisters, Sarala and Chinni (whom I called Chitti, which means "younger mother"). They lived many thousands of miles away, but through long-distance phone calls, letters we wrote back and forth, and periodic visits to India, we were always there for one another.

My mother, grandparents, aunts, and uncle instilled in Maya and me pride in our South Asian roots. Our classical Indian names harked back to our heritage, and we were raised with a strong awareness of and appreciation for Indian culture.

But my mother also understood that she was raising two black daughters. She knew that her adopted homeland would see Maya and me as black girls, and she was determined to make sure we would grow into confident, proud black women.

About a year after my parents separated, we moved into the top floor of a two-story home on Bancroft Way, in a part of Berkeley known as the flatlands. It was a close-knit neighborhood of working families who were focused on doing a good job, paying the bills, and supporting each other. It was a community that was invested in its children, a place where people believed in the most basic promise of the American Dream: that if you work hard and do right by the world, your kids will be better off than you were. We weren't rich in money, but our values provided a different kind of wealth.

My mom would get Maya and me ready every morning before heading to work at her research lab. She would kiss me goodbye and I would walk to the corner and get on the bus to Thousand Oaks Elementary School. I only learned later that we were part of a national experiment in desegregation—mixing black and white students in the classroom even if they came from neighborhoods that weren't mixed. My elementary school class was only the second class in my city to be desegregated through busing, with working-class black children from the flatlands being bused in one direction and wealthier white children from the Berkeley hills bused in the other. At the time, all I knew was that the big yellow bus was the way I got to school.

It was wonderful to grow up in such a diverse environment. I remember celebrating different cultural holidays at school and learning to count to ten in several languages. I remember parents, including my mom, volunteering in the classroom to lead science and art projects with the kids. Mrs. Frances Wilson, my first-grade teacher, loved her students. In fact, when I graduated from the University of California Hastings College of the Law, there was Mrs. Wilson sitting in the audience, cheering me on.

When Maya and I finished school for the day, our mother would often still be at work, so we would head two houses down to the Sheltons', with whom we shared a long-standing relationship of love, care, and connection.

Regina Shelton, originally from Louisiana, and her husband, Arthur, an Arkansas transplant, owned and ran a nursery school. The Sheltons were devoted to getting the children in our neighborhood off to the best possible start in life. Their day care center was small but welcoming, with posters of strong African American leaders such as Frederick Douglass, Sojourner Truth, and Harriet Tubman on the wall. The Sheltons also ran an after-school program in their home, and that's where Maya and I would spend our afternoons. We simply called it going to "the house." There were always children running around at the house; lots of laughter and joyful play.

Mrs. Shelton quickly became a second mother to Maya and me. Elegant and warm, she brought traditional southern style to her grace and hospitality—not to mention to her pound cake and flaky biscuits, which I adored. She was also deeply thoughtful in both senses of the term—exceptionally smart and uncommonly generous.

I'll never forget the time I made lemon bars to share. I had spent one afternoon making a lemon bar recipe that I'd found in one of my mother's cookbooks. They had turned out beautifully, and I was excited to show them off. I put them on a plate, covered them with plastic wrap, and walked over to Mrs. Shelton's house, where she was sitting at the kitchen table, sipping tea and laughing with her sister, Aunt Bea, and my mother. I proudly showed off my creation, and Mrs. Shelton took a big bite. It turned out I had used salt instead of sugar, but, not having tasted them myself, I didn't know.

"Mmmm, honey," Mrs. Shelton responded in her graceful southern accent, her lips slightly puckered from the taste. "That's delicious . . . maybe a little too much salt . . . but really delicious." I didn't walk away thinking I was a failure. I walked away thinking I had done a great job, and just made one small mistake. It was little moments like this that helped me build a natural sense of confidence. I believed I was capable of anything.

Mrs. Shelton taught me so much. She was always reaching out to mothers who needed counseling or support or even just a hug, because that's what you do. She took in children who couldn't live with their parents and adopted a girl named Sandy who would become my best friend. She always saw the goodness in people. I loved that about her, too. She invested in neighborhood kids who had fallen on hard times, and she did it with the expectation that these struggling boys and girls could be great. And yet she never talked about it or dwelled on it. To her, these deeds were not extraordinary; they were simply an extension of her values.

When I would come home from the Sheltons', I'd usually find my mother reading or working on her notes or preparing to make us dinner. She loved to cook, and I loved to sit with her in the kitchen and watch and smell and eat as she chopped and seasoned, mining a cupboard full of spices. We'd sing along to the music she'd play in the background.

My mother cooked like a scientist. She was always experimenting—I learned that okra could be soul food or Indian food, depending on what spices you chose; she would add dried shrimp and sausage to make it like gumbo, or fry it up with turmeric and mustard seeds. Even my lunch became a lab for her creations: On the bus, my friends, with their bologna sandwiches and PB&Js, would ask excitedly, "Kamala, what you got?" I'd open the brown paper bag, which my mother always decorated with a smiley face or a doodle: "Cream cheese and olives on dark rye!" I'll admit, not every experiment was successful—at least not for my grade school tastes. But no matter what, it was different, and that made it special, just like my mother. She even made leftovers enticing, giving them the name "smorgasbord" and setting them out with fancy toothpicks and bread cut into silly shapes. My mother had a way of making even the ordinary seem exciting.

There was a lot of laughter, too, though my mother could be tough. My sister and I rarely earned praise for behavior or achievements that were expected. "Why would I applaud you for something you were supposed to do?" she would say if I tried to fish for compliments. And if I came home to report the latest drama in search of sympathy, my mother would have none of it. Her first reaction would be: "Well, what did you do?" I guess she was trying to teach me that I had power and could make a difference. Fair enough, but it still drove me crazy.

But that toughness was always accompanied by unwavering love and loyalty and support. If Maya or I was having a bad day, or if the weather had been gray and rainy for too long, she would throw what she liked to call an "unbirthday party," with unbirthday cake and unbirthday presents. Other times, she'd make some of our favorite things—chocolate chip pancakes or her "Special K" cereal cookies ("K" for Kamala). And often, she would get out the sewing machine and make clothes for us or for our Barbie dolls. She even let Maya and me pick out the color of the family car, a Dodge Dart that she drove everywhere. We chose yellow—our favorite color at the time—and if she regretted letting us make the decision, she never let on. (On the plus side, it was always easy to find our car in a parking lot.)

On Sundays, our mother would send us off to the 23rd Avenue Church of God, piled with the other kids in the back of Mrs. Shelton's car. My earliest memories of the teachings of the Bible were of a loving God, a God who asked us to "speak up for those who cannot speak for themselves" and to "defend the rights of the poor and needy." That's why to this day I believe we must live our faith and show faith in action.

★ ★ ★

My favorite night of the week was Thursday. On Thursdays, you could always find us in a plain beige building that was bursting with life on the inside, home to a pioneering black cultural center: Rainbow Sign.

Rainbow Sign was a performance space, movie house, art gallery, dance studio, and more. It had a restaurant with a big kitchen, and somebody was always cooking up something delicious—smothered chicken, meatballs in gravy, candied yams, corn bread, peach cobbler. By day, you could take classes in dance and foreign languages, or workshops in theater and art. At night, there were movies, lectures, and performances from some of the most prominent black thinkers and leaders of the day—musicians, painters, poets, writers, filmmakers, scholars, dancers, and politicians.

My mother, Maya, and I went to Rainbow Sign often. Everyone in the neighborhood knew us as "Shyamala and the girls." We were a unit. A team. And when we'd show up at Rainbow Sign, we were always greeted with big smiles and warm hugs. Families with children were especially welcome at Rainbow Sign—an approach that reflected both the values and the vision of the women in charge of it.

This meant that kids like me who spent time at Rainbow Sign were exposed to dozens of extraordinary men and women who showed us what we could become. In 1971, Congress-woman Shirley Chisholm paid a visit while she was exploring a run for president. Talk about strength! "Unbought and Unbossed," just as her campaign slogan promised. Alice Walker, the writer who went on to win the Pulitzer Prize for *The Color Purple*, did a reading at Rainbow Sign. So did Maya Angelou, the first black female bestselling author, thanks to her autobiography, *I Know Why the Caged Bird Sings*. The singer-songwriter Nina Simone performed at Rainbow Sign when I was seven years old.

Rainbow Sign had an electric atmosphere. It was where I learned that artistic expression, ambition, and intelligence were cool. It was also where I could begin to imagine what my future might hold for me. My mother was raising us to believe that "It's too hard!" was never an acceptable excuse; that being a good person meant standing for something larger than your-self; that success is measured in part by what you help others achieve and accomplish. She would tell us, "Fight systems in a way that causes them to be fairer, and don't be limited by what has always been." It was a citizen's upbringing, the only kind I knew, and one I assumed everyone else was experiencing, too.

★ ★ ★

I was happy just where I was. But when I was in middle school, we had to leave. My mother was offered a unique opportunity in Montreal, Canada, teaching at McGill University and conducting research at the Jewish General Hospital. It was an exciting step in advancing her career.

It was not, however, an exciting opportunity for me. I was twelve years old, and the thought of moving away from sunny California in February, in the middle of the school year, to a French-speaking foreign city covered in twelve feet of snow was upsetting, to say the least. My mother tried to make it sound like an adventure, taking us to buy our first down jackets and mittens, as though we were going to be explorers of the great northern winter. But it was hard for me to see it that way. It was made worse when my mother told us that she wanted us to learn the language, so she was enrolling us in a neighborhood school for native French speakers, Notre-Dame-des-Neiges— Our Lady of the Snows.

It was a difficult transition, since the only French I knew was from my ballet classes. I used to joke that I felt like a duck, because all day long at our new school I'd be saying, "*Quoi? Quoi? Quoi?*" ("What? What? What?")

I was sure to take my upbringing with me to Montreal. One day, Maya and I held a demonstration in front of our building, protesting the fact that kids weren't allowed to play soccer on the lawn. I'm happy to report that our demands were met.

Eventually I convinced my mother to let me switch to a fine arts school, where I tried out violin, French horn, and kettle drum alongside my studies in history and math.

By the time I got to high school, I had adjusted to our new surroundings. I still missed home, my friends and family, and was always so happy to return during the summer and holidays, when we'd stay with my father or Mrs. Shelton. But I'd gotten used to most of it. What I hadn't gotten used to was the feeling of being homesick for my country. I felt this constant sense of yearning to be back home. There was no question in my mind I'd return to America for college.

During high school, I started thinking more concretely about my future—college and beyond. I'd always assumed I would have a career; I'd seen the satisfaction my parents got from their work. I'd also seen a series of extraordinary women—Aunt Mary, Mrs. Wilson, Mrs. Shelton, and my mother most of all—who were leaders making a difference in others' lives.

Though the seed was planted very early on, I'm not sure when, exactly, I decided I wanted to be a lawyer. Some of my greatest heroes were lawyers: Thurgood Marshall, Charles

Hamilton Houston, Constance Baker Motley—giants of the civil rights movement. They fought in court to make sure that people were actually treated equal in the eyes of the law, as they should be.

I cared a lot about fairness, and I saw the law as a tool that can help make things fair. But I think what most drew me to the profession was the way people around me trusted and relied on lawyers. Uncle Sherman and our close friend Henry were lawyers, and anytime someone had a problem, within the family or the neighborhood, the first thing you'd hear was "Call Henry. Call Sherman. They'll know what to do. They'll know how to make sense of this." I wanted to be able to do that. I wanted to be the one people called. I wanted to be the one who could help.

So when it came to college, I wanted to get off on the right foot. And what better place to do that, I thought, than at the university Thurgood Marshall had attended?

I had always heard stories about what a wonderful place Howard University was, especially from my mom's friend Aunt Chris, who had gone there. Howard has an extraordinary legacy, one that has lasted and grown since its founding, two years after the Civil War. It lasted when the doors of higher education were largely closed to black students. It lasted when segregation and discrimination were the law of the land. It lasted when few recognized the potential and capacity of young black men and women to be leaders. Generations of students had been nurtured and taught at Howard, equipped with the confidence to aim high and the tools to make the climb. I wanted to be one of them—and in the fall of 1982, I moved into Eton Towers, my first college dorm.

I'll always remember walking into the auditorium for my freshman orientation. The room was packed. I stood in the back, looked around, and thought, "This is heaven!" There were hundreds of people, and everyone looked like me. Some were children of Howard graduates; others were the first in their families to go to college. Some had been in predominantly black schools their whole lives; others had long been one of only a few people of color in their classroom or their neighborhood. Some came from cities, some from rural communities, and some from African countries or from the Caribbean.

As was the case for most Howard students, my favorite place to hang out was an area we called the Yard, a grass-covered space the size of a city block, right smack in the heart of the campus. On any given day, you could stand in the middle of the Yard and see, on your right, young dancers practicing their steps or musicians playing instruments. Look to your left and there were briefcase-toting students strolling out of the business school, and medical students in their white coats, heading back to the lab. Groups of students might be in a circle of laughter, or locked in deep discussion. A columnist for *The Hilltop*, the school newspaper, with the star of the football team. A gospel choir singer with the president of the math club.

That was the beauty of Howard. Every signal told students that we could be anything—that we were young, gifted, and black, as the famous Nina Simone song my mother used to play at home said, and we shouldn't let anything get in the way of our success. The campus was a place where you didn't have to be confined to the box of another person's choosing. At Howard, you could come as you were and leave as the person you hoped to be. There were no false choices.

We weren't just told we could be great; we were challenged to live up to that potential. There was an expectation that we would develop and use our talents to take on roles of leadership and have an impact on other people, on our country, and maybe even on the world.

I dove in with gusto. Freshman year, I ran for my first

elected office: freshman class representative of the Liberal Arts Student Council. It was my very first campaign.

I chaired the economics society and competed on the debate team. I pledged a sorority, Alpha Kappa Alpha, which was founded by nine women at Howard more than a century ago. And I got involved in political protests.

While at Howard, in addition to being a student, I had many jobs. Since the school was located in Washington, DC, I interned at the government agency the Federal Trade Commission. I also did research in the National Archives and was a tour guide at the U.S. Bureau of Engraving and Printing. Once, I emerged from my shift to find the legendary actors and civil rights activists Ruby Dee and Ossie Davis in the main area, waiting for a special after-hours tour. They made a point of talking to me and telling me that it made them proud to see me as a young black woman working in public service. I've never forgotten how it made me feel as a young person to have these two icons, both larger than life, take the time to show an interest in me.

In the summer of my sophomore year, I got an internship with Senator Alan Cranston of California. Who could have known that some thirty years later, I would be elected to the same Senate seat? (I still have, framed, the thank-you letter from his office manager, which hangs in my Senate office near where my own interns sit, and I often tell them, "You're looking at your future!") I loved going to the Capitol Building every day that summer for work. It felt like the epicenter of change—and even as an intern sorting mail, I was thrilled to be a part of it. But I was even more mesmerized by the Supreme Court Building, across the street. I would walk across the street in the hot, humid summer, when you could cut the air with a butter knife, just so I could stand in awe of its magnificence and read the words engraved in marble above its entrance: EQUAL JUSTICE UNDER LAW. I imagined a world where that might be.

After Howard, I returned home to Oakland and enrolled at UC Hastings College of the Law.

When I realized that I wanted to work in the district attorney's office as a prosecutor—that I had found my calling—I was excited to share the decision with my friends and family. And I wasn't surprised to find them doubtful. I had to defend my choice as if I were already in court.

Prosecutors are lawyers who work for the government and bring cases against people who commit crimes. I was interested in working as a prosecutor in the district attorney's office in Oakland—which was located in that wedding cake–like building in Alameda County in California.

America has a deep and dark history of people using the power of the prosecutor unfairly and unjustly. I knew this history well—of innocent men framed, of charges brought against people of color without enough evidence, of prosecutors hiding information that would show that defendants, those charged with a crime, were innocent. I grew up with these stories— so I understood my community's suspicions. But history told another story, too.

I knew the history of brave prosecutors who went after the racist and violent Ku Klux Klan in the South. I knew the stories of prosecutors who went after corrupt politicians and corporations that spewed pollution. I knew the legacy of Robert Kennedy, who, as U.S. attorney general, sent Department of Justice officials to protect the civil rights activists called the Freedom Riders in 1961, and sent the U.S. Marshals to protect James Meredith, the first African American student at the University of Mississippi, the next year.

I knew quite well that equal justice was a goal we hadn't met. I knew that the law was applied unevenly, sometimes on purpose. But I also knew that what was wrong with the system didn't need to be a permanent fact. And I wanted to be part of changing that.

One of my mother's favorite sayings was "Don't let

anybody tell you who you are. You tell them who you are."
And so I did. I knew part of making change was what I'd seen
all my life, surrounded by adults shouting and marching and
demanding justice from the outside. But I also knew there was
an important role on the inside, sitting at the table where the
decisions were being made. When activists came marching and
banging on the doors, I wanted to be on the other side to let
them in.

I was going to be a prosecutor in my own image. I was
going to do the job from the viewpoint of my own experiences
and perspectives, from wisdom gained at my mother's knee, in
Rainbow Sign's hall, and on the Howard Yard.

An important part of what that wisdom told me was that
when it came to criminal justice, we were being asked to accept
false choices. For too long, we'd been told there were only two
options: to be either tough on crime or soft on crime. But that
was oversimplified and it ignored the realities of public safety.
You can want the police to stop crime in your neighborhood and
also want them not to use more force than necessary. You can
want them to hunt down a killer on your streets and also want
them to stop using racial profiling, assuming people are more
likely to commit a crime because of their race, because of how
they look on the outside. You can believe that criminals should

go to prison but also stand up against jailing people unjustly.

At the end of my summer internship, I was thrilled to accept a position as deputy district attorney. All I had to do was complete my final year of law school and take the bar exam, which would certify me as an attorney who could practice law, and then I'd be able to start my career in the courtroom.

I finished law school in the spring of 1989 and took the bar exam in July. In the last weeks of summer, my future seemed so bright and so clear. The countdown to the life I imagined had begun.

And then, with a jolt, I was stopped in my tracks. In November, the state bar sent letters out to those who had taken the exam, and, to my utter devastation, I had failed. I couldn't get my head around it. It was almost too much to bear. My mother had always told me, "Don't do anything halfway," and I had always taken that to heart. I was a hard worker. A perfectionist. Someone who didn't take things for granted. But there I was, letter in hand, realizing that in studying for the bar, I had put forward the least determined performance of my life.

Fortunately, I still had a job in the district attorney's office. They were going to keep me on, with clerk duties, and give me space to study to retake the exam in February. I was grateful for that, but it was hard to go into the office, feeling like a failure. Just about everyone else who had been hired along with me had passed, and they were going to move on with their training without me. I remember walking by someone's office and hearing them say to someone else, "But she's so smart. How could she have not passed?" I felt miserable and embarrassed. I wondered if people thought I was a phony. But I held my head up and kept going to work every day—and I passed the bar exam on my second attempt. I was so proud and so honored the day I was sworn in as an officer of the court, and I showed up at the courthouse ready to start the work. But as it turns out, neither law school nor the bar exam really teach you what to do in court, and in those early days, it can feel like you've landed on another planet, where everyone speaks the language but you. And now, for the first time, I had to bring a case to trial, on my own.

I had prepared, going over the facts of the case a dozen times. I'd practiced the questions I wanted to ask over and over until I knew them by heart. I'd researched and rehearsed every procedure and custom. I'd done everything I could. Still, the stakes were so high, it never felt like enough.

I walked into the courtroom, down the main aisle, and

past the rows to the bar that separates defendants, families, witnesses, and other viewers from the officials of the court. Chairs were set up in front of the bar for lawyers waiting for their cases to be called, and I took my seat among them. I was nervous and excited. But most of all, I was honored by and very aware of the huge responsibility I held—the duty to protect those who were among the most vulnerable and voiceless members of our society. When my turn came, I rose from my chair at the prosecutor's desk and stepped up to the podium, saying the words every prosecutor speaks:

"Kamala Harris, for the people."

The reason we have public offices of prosecution in America is that, in our country, a crime against any of us is considered a crime against all of us. Almost by definition, our criminal justice system involves matters in which the powerful have harmed the less powerful, and we do not expect the weaker party to secure justice alone; we make it a group effort. That's why prosecutors don't represent the victim; they represent "the people"—all of us, society at large.

I kept that principle front and center as I worked with victims of crimes, whose dignity and safety were always the most important to me. It takes enormous courage for someone to come forward and share their story. They not only have to tell and retell about a crime that was painful or humiliating, they also have to endure cross-examination from the other side, knowing they will be questioned and that their most personal details may be on display. But when they take the stand, they are doing so for the benefit of all of us—so that there will be consequences and accountability for those who break the law.

"For the people" was my guide—and there was nothing I took more seriously than the power I now possessed. I was just starting out as a prosecutor and yet I had the ultimate say about whether to charge a defendant with a crime and, if so, what and how many charges to bring. I could make deals with the defendant's lawyer or make recommendations to a judge that could deprive a person of their freedom with the swipe of my pen.

Despite this power, our judicial system is made up of more than just the prosecutor, the defendant, and the judge. We also have a jury. Juries are twelve people who are selected from the surrounding neighborhood to listen to the cases made by lawyers on both sides and decide if the defendant is guilty or not.

When it came time for closing arguments, I approached the jury box. I decided to do it without notes so I wouldn't be looking down at a piece of paper, reading off my best arguments for why they should convict the defendant. I wanted to look the jurors in the eye. I felt that I should know my case well enough that I could close my eyes and see the entire incident in 360 degrees.

As I finished my closing and headed back to the prosecutor's table, I caught a glimpse of the audience. Amy Resner, my friend from the first day of orientation, was sitting there with a big smile on her face, cheering me on. Now we were both on our way.

The daily work was intense. At any given time, an individual prosecutor might be juggling more than one hundred cases. Eventually I was assigned to work on violent felonies—serious crimes like murder. I'd be on call for the week and have to race to the scene of a homicide when someone had been killed. Usually, that meant leaping out of bed between midnight and 6 a.m. There are rules in the U.S. Constitution for how evidence is collected and how it can be used in court. My role was to make sure it was done in the proper way. I often had to explain to victims and their families that there was a difference between what we knew happened and what we could prove happened. Just because someone is arrested for a crime doesn't mean he or she will be convicted and go to prison. The case prosecutors make depends on carefully collecting the evidence from the scene of a crime in a legal manner.

I was at home in the courtroom. I understood its rhythm. I was comfortable with its quirks. Eventually, I moved into a unit that focused on prosecuting sex crimes—putting rapists and child molesters behind bars. These are people who commit hideous crimes of sexual assault, forcing others—even kids—to perform sex acts. It was difficult, upsetting, and deeply important work. I met so many girls, and sometimes boys, who had been abused, assaulted, neglected, all too often by people they trusted.

It was hard not to feel the weight of all the big problems we were up against. Putting abusers in prison meant they wouldn't be able to hurt other children. But what about the kids they had already gotten their hands on? How had our system helped those children? That reality, and what to do about it, bounced back and forth in my head—sometimes in the back of my mind, sometimes at the front of my skull. But it would be a few years before I could tackle it head-on.

In 1998, after eight years in the Alameda County District Attorney's Office, I was recruited across the bay to the San Francisco District Attorney's Office to run the career criminal unit, which focused on violent criminals and criminals who kept committing crimes over and over again. From the moment I got there, I saw that the office was dysfunctional and had a backlog of cases.

It was rumored that when attorneys were finished with a case, some would toss the files in the trash. This was the late 1990s, and the office still didn't have email. It was an unprofessional environment and yet so powerful. It was a disgrace.

After eighteen months, I got a lifeline. The San Francisco city attorney, Louise Renne, called me with a job offer to lead the division in her office that handled child and family services. Unlike the district attorney's office, the city attorney doesn't bring criminal cases; it's basically like the law office of the city government. I told her I would take the job but that I didn't just want to be a lawyer dealing with individual cases; I wanted to work on policy that could improve the system as a whole, help kids in trouble before they ended up in the criminal justice system.

Louise was all for it.

I spent two years at the city attorney's office. I started a task force to study the issues of children who had been taken advantage of by criminals. My partner in this project was Norma Hotaling, who had a very difficult childhood but gathered the strength to turn her life around and wanted to help other kids who were facing the same kinds of challenges she had.

One of our priorities was creating a safe place for these young people to get love and support and treatment. I knew from years of experience that the survivors we were trying to help usually had nowhere to go. In most cases, their parents weren't in the picture. Many of them had run away from foster care, the temporary housing arrangements for kids who can't live with their parents. People often wondered why it was that exploited kids picked up by the police would go right back to the criminals who "took care of them." It didn't seem so strange to me—where else were these kids able to turn?

To our delight, the city government adopted and funded our recommendation to open a safe house for these kids.

The work was meaningful, empowering, and proof that I could do serious policy work. It also boosted my confidence that when I saw problems, I could be the one to help create the solutions. All those times my mother had pressed me—"Well, what did *you* do?"—suddenly made a lot more sense. I realized I didn't have to wait for someone else to take the lead; I could start making things happen on my own.

I think it was that realization that turned my sights to elected office. Of all the problems I saw in front of me, few were in more urgent need of fixing than the district attorney's office, which I had left two years prior. Suddenly it wasn't just an important problem to be solved. It was an important problem *I* could solve.

I wanted to honor, support, and empower the DA's office as a whole. But in order to run the office and make changes, I would have to run *for* elected office, because while lawyers in the DA's office aren't elected, the DA is. A political campaign would be a huge undertaking. My friends, my family, my colleagues, and my mentors were generally supportive of the idea, but they were worried, too. My would-be opponent had a reputation as a fighter; in fact, his nickname was Kayo (as in K.O., or "knockout")—a tribute to the many knockouts he scored in his boxing youth. A campaign would be not only bruising but also expensive, and I had no experience as a fund-raiser.

Was this really the time for me to run? I had no way of knowing. But more and more, I was coming to feel that "wait and see" wasn't an option. I thought of the writer James Baldwin, whose words had defined so much of the civil rights struggle. "There is never a time in the future in which we will work out our salvation," he'd written. "The challenge is in the moment; the time is always now."

Two

A VOICE FOR JUSTICE

K amala, let's go. Come on, we're going to be late." My mother was losing patience. "Just a second, Mommy," I called back. (Yes, my mother was and always will be "Mommy" to me.) We were on our way to campaign headquarters, where volunteers were gathering. My mother often took charge of the volunteer operation, and she didn't dillydally. Everyone knew that when Shyamala spoke, you listened.

We drove from my apartment and past the wealth and attractions of San Francisco's downtown to a mostly black neighborhood in the southeast part of town known as Bayview–Hunters Point. The Bayview had been home to the Hunters Point Naval Shipyard, which helped to build America's fighting fleet in the mid-twentieth century. In the 1940s, the prospect of good jobs and affordable housing around the shipyard lured thousands of black Americans who were seeking opportunity and relief from the pain and injustice of segregation. These workers bent the steel and welded the plates that helped our nation win the Second World War.

But like too many similar neighborhoods in America, the Bayview was no longer thriving. After the shipyard closed, people struggled to find jobs. Beautiful old houses were boarded up; toxic waste polluted the soil, water, and air; drugs and violence poisoned the streets; and poverty of the worst kind settled in for the long haul. The Bayview was the kind of place that no one in the city ever saw unless they made it their business to go there. You didn't pass it on the freeway. You didn't cross it to get from one part of the city to another. It was, in deeply tragic ways, invisible to the world beyond it. I wanted to be a part of changing that. So I headquartered my campaign for district attorney right in the heart of the Bayview.

The political consultants thought I was nuts. They said no campaign volunteers would ever come to the Bayview from other parts of the city. But it was places like the Bayview that had inspired me to run in the first place. I wasn't running so I could have a fancy office downtown. I was running for the chance to represent people whose voices weren't being heard, and to bring the promise of public safety to every neighborhood, not just some. Besides, I didn't believe that people wouldn't come to the Bayview. And I was right: They did come. By the dozens.

San Francisco, like our country as a whole, is diverse yet deeply segregated—more mosaic than melting pot. Yet our campaign attracted people representing the full vibrancy of the whole community: white, black, Asian, and Latinx; wealthy and working-class; male and female; old and young; gay and straight. A group of teenage graffiti artists decorated the back wall of campaign headquarters, spray-painting JUSTICE in giant letters. HQ buzzed with volunteers, some calling voters, some sitting together around a table stuffing envelopes, others picking up clipboards so they could go door-to-door talking to people in the community about what we were trying to do.

We pulled up to headquarters just in time. I let my mother out. "You have the ironing board?" she asked.

"Yeah, of course, it's in the back seat."

"Okay. I love you," she said as she shut the car door.

As I drove away, I could hear her call, "Kamala, what about the duct tape?"

I had the duct tape.

I got back on the road and drove toward the nearest supermarket. It was a Saturday morning, the equivalent of rush hour in the grocery aisles. I pulled into the parking lot, snuck my car into one of the few open spots, and grabbed the ironing board, the tape, and a campaign sign that looked slightly worn from being tossed in and out of the car.

If you think running for office sounds glamorous, I wish you could have seen me striding through the parking lot with an ironing board under my arm. I remember the kids who would look curiously at the ironing board and point, and the moms who would hustle them past. I couldn't blame them. I must have looked out of place—if not totally out of my mind.

But an ironing board makes for the perfect standing desk. I set it up in front of the supermarket entrance, just off to the side, near the carts, and taped up a sign that read KAMALA HARRIS, A VOICE FOR JUSTICE. I put several stacks of my flyer on the ironing board and, next to it, a clipboard with a sign-up sheet. Then I got to work.

Shoppers rolled their carts out the automatic doors, squinting at the sunlight, trying to remember where they parked the car. And then, out of left field, I'd say:

"Hi! I'm Kamala Harris. I'm running for district attorney, and I hope to have your support."

In truth, I would have settled for them just remembering my name. Early on in the campaign, we did a poll to see how many people in the county of San Francisco had heard of me. The answer was a whopping 6 percent. As in six of every one hundred people had heard of me before. I couldn't help but wonder: Was my mother one of the people they'd randomly called?

But I hadn't gotten into this thinking it would be easy. I knew I'd have to work hard to introduce myself and what I stood for to a whole lot of people who had no idea who I was.

For some first-time candidates, interacting with strangers can feel awkward, and understandably so. It isn't easy to start a conversation with someone who passes you on the street, or to try to connect with them at the bus stop on their way home after work, or to walk into a merchant's business and try to strike up a conversation with the owner. I got my share of polite—and occasionally not so polite—snubs. But more often than not, I met people who were welcoming, open, and eager to talk about the issues affecting their daily lives and their hopes for their family and their community. Years later, I still run into people who remember our interactions at those bus stops.

It may sound strange, but the thing it reminded me of most was jury selection for a court case. When I worked as a prosecutor, I spent a lot of time in the courtroom, talking to people who'd been called for jury duty from every part of the community. My job was to ask them questions over the course of a few minutes and, based on that, try to figure out what was important to them. Campaigning was kind of like that, but without the lawyer from the other side trying to cut me off. I loved being able to talk to people. Sometimes a mom would come out of the grocery store with a toddler in the shopping cart seat, and we'd find ourselves spending a good twenty minutes talking about her life, and her struggles, and her daughter's Halloween costume. Before we parted, I'd look her in the eye and say, "I hope I can have your support." It's amazing how often people would tell me that no one had ever asked them that directly before.

Still, this process didn't come naturally to me. I was always more than happy to talk about the work to be done. But voters wanted to hear about more than just policy. They wanted to know about me personally—who I was, what my life had been like, the experiences that had shaped me. They wanted to understand who I was down deep. But I'd been raised not to talk about myself. I'd been raised with the belief that there was something vain about doing so. And so, even though I understood what was motivating their questions, it took some time before I got used to it.

There were multiple candidates in my first DA's race, and a runoff was inevitable. This meant that after Election Day, the top two vote getters would face each other in a second election weeks later.

I spent Election Day on the streets shaking hands, from the predawn commute until the polls closed. My family, friends, senior campaign staff members, and I went out to dinner as the results started rolling in. With each voting precinct that reported, and between bites of pasta, they would update the tally on the paper tablecloth.

We were getting ready to leave when my sister, Maya, grabbed my arm. A new update had come in.

"Oh, my God, you did it!" she exclaimed. "You made the runoff!"

I did the math myself to make sure she was right. I remember looking at Maya and Maya looking at me and both of us saying, "Can you believe it—we're really in this!"

The runoff was held five weeks later. It rained that day, and I spent it getting soaked as I shook hands with voters at bus stops. That night, as I'd hoped, we won a decisive victory.

We held a party at campaign headquarters, and I walked out to speak as "We Are the Champions" blasted through the room. Looking out at the crowd—friends, family, mentors, volunteers from the campaign—I saw one community. There were people from the poorest neighborhoods and the richest.

Police officers alongside advocates fighting for police reform. Young people cheering with senior citizens. It was a reflection of what I've always believed to be true: when it comes to the things that matter most, we have so much more in common than what separates us.

For my inauguration ceremony for district attorney, the room was packed to overflowing, filled with hundreds of people from all corners of the city. Drummers drummed. A youth choir sang. One of my pastors said a beautiful prayer. Chinese dragon dancers roamed the aisles. The San Francisco Gay Men's Chorus serenaded us all. It was multicultural, multi-racial, a little frenzied in all the best and most beautiful ways.

After my swearing-in, I made my way through the crowd, shaking hands and getting hugs and taking in the joy of it all. As the festivities were winding down, a man came up to me with his two young daughters.

"I brought them here today," he said, "so they could see what someone who looked like them could grow up to do."

After the inauguration, I snuck away to see my new office. I wanted to know what it felt like to sit in the chair. My staff member Debbie Mesloh and I drove to the Hall of Justice.

Standing right next to the freeway, "850," as it was known (for 850 Bryant Street), was a gray, solemn, and imposing building; I used to joke that it was a "horribly wonderful" place to work. In addition to the district attorney's office, the building housed the police department, the criminal courts, the city tow office, the county jail, and the city coroner's office, where homicides were investigated. There was no doubt this was a place where people's lives were changed, sometimes forever.

"Oh, wow." I surveyed my office. Or, more accurately, I looked around the empty room. It had been stripped of almost everything as part of the transition. A metal cabinet sat against one wall with a 1980s Wang computer on top of it. (Mind you, it was 2004.) No wonder the office hadn't gotten email yet. A plastic-lined wastebasket stood in the corner; a few loose wires stuck out of the floor. There was no desk in the office, just a chair where the desk had been. But that was okay. It was the chair I had come for. I took my seat.

Now it was quiet. And for the first time since the day began, I was alone with my thoughts, taking it all in.

I had run because I knew I could do the job—and I believed I could do it better than it had been done. Still, I knew I represented something much bigger than my own experience. At the time, there weren't many district attorneys who looked like me or had my background. There still aren't. A report in 2015 found that more than nine out of ten of our country's elected prosecutors were white, and about eight in ten were white men.

No part of me would more fully inform my perspective than the decade I had spent as a prosecutor. I knew the criminal justice system backward and forward. For what it was, for what it wasn't, and for what it could be. The courthouse was supposed to be the epicenter of justice; but it was often a great epicenter of injustice. I knew both to be true.

I had been around the courtroom long enough to see victims of violence show up years later as people who committed violence against others. I worked with children who had grown up in neighborhoods so crime ridden that their stress levels were as high as those growing up in war zones. I had worked with kids in foster care who changed homes six times before turning eighteen. I had seen children marked for a bleak future solely because they came from high-crime neighborhoods. Of course lawbreakers should be punished, but didn't the kids and families in these communities also deserve help when they fell down?

Instead, our system was designed to lock people up. The United States puts more people in prison than any country in the world. All told, we had more than 2.1 million people locked up in state and federal prisons in 2018. To put that in perspective: there are fifteen American states that have smaller populations than that. Many were imprisoned because a police officer found them with illegal drugs.

Early in my career, I was assigned to a part of the Alameda County DA's office known as the bridge, where lawyers in small offices would handle drug cases by the hundreds. There were bad actors in the piles, to be sure, plenty of drug dealers selling to kids or forcing kids to sell for them. But too many case files told a different story: a man arrested for carrying a small amount of drugs; a woman arrested on her front stoop for being "under the influence" of drugs. Even for a relatively minor offense, these people were facing a lot of jail time.

The truth is that there are communities in America that have very few jobs and very bad schools and very high crime and very few chances for people to succeed. And in places like that, drug addiction spreads like a wildfire raging out of control. But what people refused to accept was that drug addiction is a disease, and the best way to cure a disease is with good medical treatment. Instead, our system threw people who were struggling with addiction into jail.

As I sat alone in my new office, I recalled a time, as a

young prosecutor, when I overheard some of my colleagues in the hallway.

"Can we show he was in a gang?" one of them asked.

"Come on, you saw what he was wearing, you saw which corner they picked him up on. Guy's blasting the music of that rapper, what's his name?"

I stepped out into the hallway. "Hey, guys, just so you know: I have family that live in that neighborhood. I've got friends who dress in that style. And I've got a recording of that rapper in my car right now." I reflected on it all—about why I ran for office, whom I had come there to help, and the difference between getting convictions and having conviction. In the end, I knew I was there for the victims. Both the victims of crimes committed and the victims of a broken criminal justice system.

For me, to be a progressive prosecutor is to understand—and act on—these two ideas at the same time. When a child is abused, or a woman killed by her partner, the perpetrators, those who commit the crimes, must be punished. But I also wanted to get to the core of the problem—what sets off criminal behavior? Can we make a difference for the better in the lives of troubled people before they ever commit a crime, so they don't get caught up in the justice system in the first place?

I saw my role as shining a light on the inequality and unfairness that lead to injustice. As recognizing that not everyone needs punishment, that what many need, quite plainly, is help.

There was a knock at the door. It was my staffer Debbie. "You ready?" she asked, smiling.

"I'll be there in a second," I told her. I breathed in the silence for another moment. Then I pulled a pen and a yellow notepad from my briefcase and started to make a list.

I had just sat down at my desk when my assistant came in. "Boss, there's another mom out here."

"Thanks, I'll be right out."

I walked down the hallway to the lobby to greet her. I'd been on the job only a few weeks, but it was not the first time I'd taken this walk. This was not the first time a woman had shown up and said, "I want to speak to Kamala. I will only speak to Kamala." I knew exactly why she was there. She was the mother of a murdered child.

The woman nearly collapsed in my arms. She was grieving and exhausted. And yet her being there showed how strong she was. She was there for her baby, the baby she'd lost, a young man killed by gunfire in the streets. It had been months since her son's death, and yet the killer still walked free. The case was one of the more than seventy unsolved homicides collecting dust in the San Francisco Police Department when I took office. I had known some of these mothers, and others I had met while I was campaigning. They were almost all black or Latina from high-crime neighborhoods, and all of them loved their children deeply. They had come together to form a group, Mothers of Homicide Victims. It was part support group, part advocacy organization. They leaned on one another to work through their grief. And they organized to get justice for their sons.

They weren't sure if I could help them, but they knew that I would at least see them. See their pain, see their anguish, see their souls—which were bleeding. First and foremost, they knew I would see them as loving, grieving mothers.

This is part of the tragedy. When people hear that a mother has lost a child to cancer or a car accident or war, the natural response is collective sympathy and concern. But when a woman loses her son to violence in the streets, the response from the public is often different, almost a collective shrug, as though it was expected to happen. Not the horrific tragedy of losing a child, but rather just another statistic. As though the circumstances of her son's death define the value of his life. As though the loss she has suffered is less valid, less painful, less worthy of compassion.

I walked her back to my office so we could have some privacy to talk. She told me her son had been shot and killed, that no one had been arrested, that no one seemed to care. She described the day she had to identify his dead body—how she couldn't get that image out of her head, of him lifeless in a place so cold. She had left messages for the homicide inspector, she said, suggesting possible leads, but she never heard back. Nothing had happened, nothing seemed to be happening, and she couldn't understand why. She grasped my hand and looked me straight in the eye. "He mattered," she said. "He still matters to me."

"He matters to me, too," I reassured her. His life should have mattered to everyone. I told my team to get the entire squad of homicide inspectors to meet in my conference room as soon as possible. I wanted to know what was going on with all of these cases.

The homicide inspectors showed up not knowing what to expect. At the time I didn't know it was uncommon for the district attorney to gather them for a meeting. One by one, I asked them to tell me the status of the unresolved homicide cases and pressed them for details about what they were going to do to help us get justice for these families. I had very pointed questions, and I pushed the inspectors hard—harder, I later learned, than they were expecting. This made some people angry. But it was the right thing to do, and it needed to be done—regardless of whether it had ever been done before.

They took my call to action seriously. Within a month of the meeting, the police department launched a new campaign to try to encourage witnesses to step forward. And in time, we were able to reduce the backlog of unsolved homicides by 25 percent. Not every case could be solved, but we worked hard to ensure that every one that could be was.

Some people were surprised I was so persistent. And I know some others questioned how I, as a black woman, could be part of "the machine" putting more young men of color behind bars. There is no doubt that the criminal justice system has deep flaws, that it is broken in fundamental ways. And we need to deal with that. But we cannot overlook or ignore that mother's pain, that child's death, that murderer who still walks the streets. I believe there must be serious consequences for people who commit serious crimes.

But let's be clear: the situation is not the same—nor should it be—when it comes to less serious crimes. I remember the first time I visited the county jail. So many young men, and they were mostly black or brown or poor. Too many were there because of addiction to drugs and desperation and poverty. They were fathers who missed their kids. They were young adults, many of whom had been pulled into gangs with no real choice in the matter. People whose lives had been destroyed, along with their families and their communities. These were the faces of a system that jails too many for nonviolent offenses. They represented a living monument to lost potential, and I wanted to tear it down.

In 1977, in the heart of the San Francisco neighborhood known as Western Addition, my friend Lateefah Simon was born. She grew up in what was once a middle-class neighborhood as an epidemic was starting to take hold—an epidemic of people getting addicted to a drug called crack. She saw, firsthand, that it was ruining her community. When Lateefah was a young girl, she wanted to help people, but as she got older, she became one of the many who needed help. She ended up on probation for shoplifting, so she didn't have to go to jail, but was monitored closely to stay out of trouble. She dropped out of high school.

But then someone intervened. Lateefah was a teenager, working eight hours a day at Taco Bell, when an outreach

worker told her about an opportunity. There was an organization in San Francisco, the Center for Young Women's
Development, that provided social services, including job
training, to girls and young women who were on the streets or
in trouble. The center was looking for new staff to work there.
Lateefah saw a lifeline and grabbed hold.

She started working for the center when she was a teenager
and raising a daughter of her own; soon she was unstoppable.
She was everywhere: at local government meetings, calling for
changes to help girls who were being abused; on the streets of
poor neighborhoods handing out candy bars, along with information about how to get help; and at the center itself, working
with vulnerable girls from her neighborhood. "I saw resilience
in these young women," she said. "There were people who had
absolutely nothing but were somehow able to make it through
the day. And the next day. And the next."

The center's board members were so impressed by
Lateefah's hard work, skills, and leadership that they asked her
to become executive director when she was just nineteen years
old. She said yes—and that was when I came to know her.

At the city attorney's office, I had been working with the
same community of women that Lateefah had. I had been
holding "know your rights" sessions for vulnerable women all

across the city, and I asked Lateefah to join our efforts. I could see that Lateefah was a genius.

When I became district attorney, I often thought to myself, "What if Lateefah had been picked up for drugs instead of shoplifting?" Instead of probation, she'd have ended up in prison, facing huge obstacles afterward. In America, we release inmates into desperate, hopeless situations. We give them a little bit of money and a bus ticket and we send them on their way with a felony conviction on their record. Employers don't want to hire them, so they have no way of making money. From the moment they leave prison, they are in danger of returning. They end up in the same neighborhood, with the same people, on the same corner; the only difference is that they've now served time. Prison has its own gravitational pull, often inescapable; of the hundreds of thousands of prisoners we release as a country every year, nearly 70 percent commit a crime within three years.

What could we do to prevent people from reoffending, or committing crimes again?

What if we could really get them back on track?

That question would become the name of the program my team and I developed together: Back on Track. At the heart of the program was my belief in the power of redemption.

Redemption is an age-old concept rooted in many religions. It is a concept that assumes that we will all make mistakes, and for some, that mistake will rise to the level of being a crime. Yes, there must be punishment; we have to be held accountable for our actions. But after that, is it not the sign of a civil society that we allow people to earn their way back?

We had to imagine what that would look like and how it would work. For a lot of the people in the program, they'd committed crimes because they'd never had a support system to help them navigate life—all sorts of basics that I could take for granted because they were a part of my upbringing. What would people need to lead good, comfortable lives and keep from committing crimes? They'd need good jobs. Most good jobs depend on training and schooling, so they'd need that too. If they were addicted to drugs, they'd need help getting off them. Once they had a good job that they could attend regularly because they were clean from drugs, they'd need counseling to know how to manage the money they made so that they could figure out how much to spend on rent and food and clothes, and how much they could save for their futures.

Though compassionate in its approach, Back on Track was intense, too. Participants had to first plead guilty to the crimes they had committed—for this program, we only worked with people charged with nonviolent crimes—and accept responsibility for the actions that had brought them there. We promised that if participants completed the program successfully, we would have their charges cleared, which gave them even more reason to put in the effort. We designed a program that was about transformation. We knew what these young people were capable of achieving—and we wanted them to see it in themselves. We wanted every participant to reach for the highest bar.

When it came time to identify someone to run the program, one name immediately came to mind. I called Lateefah.

At first, she didn't want to. She had never imagined herself as the kind of person who would work for the DA. "I never wanted to work for the Man," she told me.

"Well, don't worry," I laughed. "You won't be working for the Man. You'll be working for me."

Lateefah worked incredibly hard. And so did the Back on Track students. And on a night I'll never forget, we got to share in the fruits of that effort together.

My chief of policy, Tim Silard, who had helped develop Back on Track, joined me, Lateefah, and many others from my office after the court had closed for the evening. We headed down the hall toward the jury assembly room. When we entered, the room was filled with people carrying flowers and balloons. The bustling, joyous mood was not typical in a jury room, to say the least. But this was not a typical night. I walked to the front of the room and opened the ceremonies for the first Back on Track graduation ceremony.

Through the main door, a group of eighteen men and women walked down the aisle to take their seats. With few exceptions, this was the first time in their lives they had ever worn graduation robes. Only a handful of them had ever had a chance to invite their family to an event that would make their loved ones cry happy tears. This celebration was hard-won, and they deserved every minute of it. They had all earned a high school degree, landed jobs, were drug-free, and had completed community service.

In exchange for that hard work and that success, we were there to keep our promise. In addition to a diploma, the graduates would have their records cleared by a judge who was standing by.

Back on Track quickly proved its worth. After two years, only 10 percent of Back on Track graduates had reoffended—compared with half of others convicted of similar crimes who hadn't been through Back on Track. And it was less expensive, too. Prosecuting a felony case costs twice as much, and putting up someone in jail for a year costs another eight times as much.

When I ran for attorney general of California a few years later, I did so, in no small part, to take the program statewide.

Whenever we held a Back on Track graduation during my time as DA, we'd make sure that current program participants were there to see what their future could hold. And whenever I spoke at those ceremonies, I'd tell the graduates what I knew to be true: that the program depended a lot more on them than on us. This accomplishment was theirs, and I wanted to make sure they knew it. But I wanted them to know that it was also bigger than themselves.

"People are watching you," I'd tell them. "They are watching you. And when they see your success, they'll think, 'Maybe we can do that, too. Maybe we should try it back home.' You should feel inspired by that, by knowing that your success here will someday create an opportunity for someone you've never met before in some other part of the country."

When I first started as DA and I took out that notepad and made a to-do list, there was a lot I wanted to get done, a lot that needed to get done. I wanted to make sure I wrote it all down. I even included "Paint the walls." I was serious, too. I've always believed there is no problem too small to fix. I know it may sound silly, but people were working in offices that hadn't been painted in years. It was depressing for the staff.

Painting was simple. But the larger goal was restoring professionalism as the highest value—making sure everyone knew that skills and hard work were important. I knew that there was a direct link between professionalizing the office and making sure it delivered justice.

Professionalism, as I see it, is in part about what happens inside an office. But it's also about how people carry themselves outside the office. When I trained younger lawyers, I'd say, "Let's be clear. You represent the people. So I expect you to get to know exactly who the people are." I'd tell my team to learn about the communities where they didn't live, to follow neighborhood news, to go to local festivals and community forums. "For the people" means for them. All of them. At stake was justice itself. A broken DA's office leads to injustice. Prosecutors are human beings; when they are not at their best, they do not perform their best—and that could mean people who should go to prison walk free and people who shouldn't go to prison end up behind bars. Such is the power prosecutors have.

I had divided my to-do list into three categories: short-, medium-, and long-term. Short-term meant "a couple of weeks," medium-term meant "a couple of years," and long-term meant "as long as it takes." It was that far side of the ledger where I wrote down the hardest problems we were facing—the ones you can't expect to solve on your own, over a term in office, perhaps even over a career. That's where the most important work is. That's where you take the bigger view—not of the political moment but of the historical one. The core problems of the criminal justice system are not new. You don't add the toughest problems to the list because they are new, but because they are big, because people have been fighting against them for dozens—maybe even hundreds—of years, and that duty is now yours. What matters is how well you run the portion of the race that is yours.

It was my mother who had taught me that. I grew up surrounded by people who were battling for civil rights and equal justice. But I had also seen it in her work. My mother was a breast cancer researcher. Like her colleagues, she dreamed of the day we'd find a cure. But in her daily tasks, she focused on the work right in front of her. The work that would move us closer, day by day, year by year, until we crossed the finish line. "Focus on what's in front of you and the rest will follow," she would say.

That is the spirit we need to bring to building a more perfect union: realizing that we are part of a longer story, and we are responsible for how our chapter gets written. In the battle to build a smarter, fairer, more effective criminal justice system, there is an enormous amount of work to do. We know what the problems are. So let's roll up our sleeves and start fixing them.

One of the key issues I focused on during my first year in the Senate was the country's bail system—the process by which you can be released from jail while you await trial after you've been charged with a crime.

In this country, when you are arrested by the police you are innocent until proven guilty. Unless you are a danger to others or highly likely to run away and not show up for your trial, you shouldn't have to sit in jail waiting for your court date. This is the basic premise of due process: you get to hold on to your freedom unless and until a jury convicts you—finds you guilty—and a judge sentences you with the appropriate punishment, which may include time in prison. It's why the Bill of Rights clearly forbids excessive bail. That's what justice is supposed to look like.

What it should not look like is the system we have in America today. The median bail in the United States is $10,000, which is four times the savings many Americans have in their bank accounts. Roughly nine out of ten people who are detained can't afford to pay to get out.

By its very design, the cash bail system favors the wealthy and punishes the poor. If you can pay cash up front, you can leave, and when your trial is over, you'll get all of your money back. If you can't afford it, you are forced to suffer in jail. The only other option is to get a bail bondsman to pay your bail, but they charge steep fees you will never get back.

When I was district attorney, I knew that every day, families were leaving the Hall of Justice, crossing the street, walking into bail bonds offices, having done whatever it took to get the cash to pay the bondsmen their fees—selling their belongings, getting loans which demanded their own steep fees, asking for help from their friends or at church. I also knew that people who were likely to win their cases instead admitted guilt under the pressure of facing jail time. At least if they took these guilty pleas, they could get out of jail and back to their job or home to their kids.

The New York Times Magazine told the story of a struggling single mother who spent two weeks on Rikers Island, New York City's enormous jail, arrested and charged with endangering the welfare of a child, because she'd left her baby with a friend at a shelter while she bought diapers at Target. This young woman could not afford her $1,500 bail, and by the time she was released, her child was in foster care. In another case, sixteen-year-old Kalief Browder was arrested in New York on charges that he had stolen a backpack. When his family couldn't scrape together the $3,000 bail, Kalief went to jail while he awaited his trial. He would end up spending the next three years waiting, endlessly waiting, much of it in solitary confinement—trapped in an isolated jail cell with almost no human contact—not having ever been tried or convicted of anything. It was a tragic story from beginning to end: in 2015, soon after he was finally released from jail, Kalief committed suicide.

The criminal justice system punishes people for their poverty. Where is the justice in that? And where is the sense? How does that improve public safety? Between 2000 and 2014, 95 percent of the growth in the jail population came from people awaiting trial. This is a group of largely nonviolent defendants who haven't been proven guilty, and we're spending $38 million a day to imprison them while they await their day in court. Whether or not someone can get bailed out of jail shouldn't be based on how much money he has in the bank. Or the color of his skin: black men pay 35 percent higher bail than white men charged with the same crime. Latino men pay nearly 20 percent more than white men. This isn't the stuff of coincidences. It runs deep in the system. And we have to change it.

In 2017, I introduced a bill in the Senate to encourage states to replace their bail systems. If someone poses a threat to the public, we should keep them in jail. If someone is likely to flee, we should keep them in jail. But if not, we shouldn't be in the business of charging people money in exchange for their freedom.

We also need to stop jailing people who are addicted to drugs instead of helping them. It's time that we all accept that addiction is a disease, that it wrecks people's lives in ways they don't want and never intended. It's time we recognize that addiction harms everyone it touches, no matter the color of their skin or the size of their bank account. Addiction does not discriminate, and our laws shouldn't either. When someone is suffering from addiction, their situation is made worse, not better, by involvement in the criminal justice system. What they need is treatment, and we should fight for a system that provides it.

And even when people have committed offenses that require jail time, that doesn't mean they'll never do right or that they don't deserve a second chance. And yet, judges often must follow harsh and strict guidelines when sentencing those convicted of crimes, guidelines that often are discriminatory against people of color.

Thankfully, we have started to see progress: In the decade after we introduced Back on Track, some thirty-three states have adopted new sentencing and corrections policies that aim to provide alternatives to prison and reduce recidivism, the likelihood that people will commit new crimes and land back in jail. And since 2010, twenty-three states have reduced their prison populations. But there is still much more work to do to ensure that punishments match the crimes committed.

We also need to address what happens behind the prison gates. Women are now the fastest-growing segment of our incarcerated population. Most of them are mothers, and the vast majority have experienced violence. Many still suffer the effects. Many are imprisoned in facilities that don't support their hygiene and health. As you read this, there are women being shackled while they're pregnant. In some states, they are shackled while giving birth. I have visited women in prison, heard stories of the risks of violence they face when supervised by male guards in the bathroom or shower. In 2017, I was proud to co-sponsor a bill to deal with some of these issues. This is a conversation we rarely have in this country—and we need to.

In the near term, one of the most urgent challenges is the fight against the current administration, which is ripping apart the critical progress we've made in recent years to reform the criminal justice system. We can't go backward on these issues when we have only begun to scratch the surface of progress. We have to act with fierce urgency. Justice demands it.

One thing we must do is take on the racial bias—the prejudice—in our criminal justice system. And that effort starts with our stating clearly that black lives matter—and speaking truth about what that means. The facts are clear: Across the nation, when a police officer stops a black driver, he is three times more likely to search the car than when the driver is white. Black men use drugs at the same rate as white men, but they are arrested twice as often for it. Black men are six times as likely as white men to be incarcerated, or jailed. And when they are convicted, black men get prison sentences nearly 20 percent longer than those given to white men who committed the same crimes. Latino men don't fare much better. It is truly appalling.

It's one thing to say that black lives matter. But we need to accept hard truths about the long-running racism that has allowed this to happen. And we need to turn that understanding into policies and practices that can actually change it.

One critical way to do that is to confront implicit bias, the unconscious shortcuts our brains use to help us make a quick judgment about a stranger at first sight. When I was attorney general, I committed to training our agents on implicit bias. Frontline officers, more than most, have to make split-second judgments all the time, where implicit bias can have a deadly outcome.

It was a hard topic to tackle. The senior leaders I was working with had dedicated their lives and taken an oath to law enforcement. It wasn't easy to have to accept the idea that the men and women of their bureau carry bias with them, that it affects the community, and that they need to be trained to deal with it. But it was an honest conversation, and in the end, the leadership not only agreed it was important, but they also agreed to help create, shape, and lead the training.

My team got to work, and it became the first statewide implicit bias and procedural justice course offered anywhere in the country.

None of us were naive about what our training course could accomplish. We knew that such an effort, alone, would not rid the system of bias. And we surely knew that the system was infected by explicit bias, too. Racism is real in America, and police departments are not immune. At the same time, we knew that better training would make a real difference, that for most members of law enforcement, a better understanding of their own implicit biases could be meaningful. We knew that the hard conversations involved in the training course were the kind that stayed with a person, the kind of thing they'd take with them to the streets.

We need to speak another truth: police brutality—police using excess force—occurs in America and we have to root it out wherever we find it. What was well known only to certain communities is now being seen by the world, thanks to smartphones capturing some of these events. People can no longer pretend it isn't happening. It cannot be ignored or denied when we see video of Walter Scott, unarmed, shot in the back as he ran from an officer. We cannot ignore the horrified cries of Philando Castile's girlfriend after he was shot seven times by a police officer while reaching for his driver's license—all with her four-year-old daughter in the back seat. "It's okay, Mommy . . . it's okay. I'm right here with you," the little girl said, in a heartbreaking attempt to comfort. We cannot forget Eric Garner's desperate words—"I can't breathe"—as a police officer strangled him to death during an arrest for selling cigarettes.

And we must remember that tragedies like these occur over and over again, most of them unfilmed and unseen. If people fear murder and beatings and harassment from the police who patrol their streets, can we really say that we live in a free society?

And what does it say about our standards of justice when police officers are so rarely held accountable for these incidents? The Minnesota officer who shot Philando Castile faced trial and was not convicted. In Ohio, a police officer climbed onto the hood of a car after a car chase and fired forty-nine times inside at Timothy Russell and Malissa Williams, both of whom were unarmed. The officer was charged—and cleared of a crime. In Pennsylvania, a police officer shot an unarmed driver in the back while he lay facedown in the snow. But he, too, was acquitted—not convicted—of murder.

If there aren't serious penalties for police brutality in our justice system, what kind of message does that send to police officers? And what kind of message does it send to the community? Public safety depends on public trust. It depends on people believing they will be treated fairly and transparently. It depends on the basic decency our Constitution demands.

But when black and brown people are more likely to be stopped, arrested, and convicted than white people; when police departments are outfitted like military battalions; when deadly force is overused, is it any wonder that people have stopped trusting these public institutions?

I say this as someone who has spent most of my career working with law enforcement. I say this as someone who has a great deal of respect for police officers. I know that most police officers deserve to be proud of their public service and commended for the way they do their jobs. I know how difficult and dangerous the job is, day in and day out, and I know how hard it is for the officers' families, who have to wonder if the person they love will be coming home at the end of each shift. I've been to too many funerals of officers killed in the line of duty. But I also know this: it is a false choice to suggest that you must either be for the police or for responsible policing. I am for both. Most people I know are for both. Let's speak some truth about that, too.

Make no mistake: we need to take on this and every aspect of our broken criminal justice system. We need to pay attention to activists who demand justice. We need to change our laws and our standards. And we need to elect people who will make it their mission to do so.

So let's recruit more progressives into prosecutors' offices, where many of the biggest problems and best solutions start. Prosecutors are among the most powerful actors in our system of justice. They have the power to put criminals behind bars, but they also have the choice to dismiss cases where police used excessive force, or carried out a search improperly. We need people who come from all walks of life and different backgrounds and experiences to sit at the table and use that kind of power.

We also need to keep the pressure on from outside the prosecutors' offices, where organizations and individuals can create meaningful change. When I was attorney general, I made sure ours was the first state law enforcement agency to require body cameras for its agents. This policy would record every interaction the agents had with members of the public, so we'd know if excess force had been used. I did it because it was the right thing to do. But I was able to do it because protestors had created intense pressure. The Black Lives Matter movement, which includes organizations and activists who oppose police violence and demand justice, created an environment on the outside that helped give me the space to get it done on the inside. That's often how change happens. And I credit the movement for those reforms just as much as anyone in my office, including me.

The fight for civil rights and social justice is not for the faint of heart. It is as difficult as it is important, and the wins may never taste as sweet as the losses taste sour. But count yourself as part of a long line of people who refused to give up. And when we're feeling frustrated and discouraged by the obstacles in front of us, let's channel the words of Constance Baker Motley, one of my inspirations as the first black American woman appointed as a federal judge. "Lack of encouragement never deterred me," she wrote. "In fact, I think the effect was just the opposite. I was the kind of person who would not be put down."

Three

UNDERWATER

My mother took incredible pride in our home. It was always ready for company, with fresh-cut flowers. The walls were decorated with big posters of artwork from the Studio Museum in Harlem, where my uncle Freddy worked. There were statues from her travels in India, Africa, and elsewhere. She cared a lot about making our apartment a home, and it always felt warm and complete. But I knew my mother always wanted something more.

When it comes to housing, most people either rent or own a home. We were renters for most of my childhood. A landlord owned our home and we paid money every month to live there. Homes are expensive, so if a family owns one, they probably borrowed money from the bank to buy it. This loan is called a mortgage. Instead of paying rent to a landlord, most homeowners pay back a little bit of the loan each month.

My mother always wanted to be a homeowner.

She would be the first to point out that it was a smart investment. But it was so much more than that. It was about her earning a full slice of the American Dream.

My mother had wanted to buy her first home while Maya and I were still young—a place to grow up with a sense of permanence. But it would take many years before she could save up enough money for a down payment, the big chunk of money that you pay for the home along with the loan you get from the bank.

I was in high school when it happened. Maya and I had just gotten home from school when she pulled out the pictures to show us—a one-level dark-gray house with a shingled roof, a beautiful lawn in front, an outdoor space on the side for a barbecue. She was so excited to show us, and we were so excited to see it—not only because it meant we got to move back to Oakland, but because of the intense joy we saw in her face. She had earned it, quite literally. "This is our house!" I would tell my friends, proudly showing off the pictures. It was going to be our piece of the world.

That memory was on my mind when I traveled to Fresno, California, in 2010, in the midst of a devastating crisis in which so many people had their own piece of the world destroyed—they lost their homes because they could no longer afford their mortgages.

Fresno is the largest city in California's San Joaquin Valley, an area that has been described as the "Garden of the Sun." The San Joaquin Valley grows a huge share of the fruits and vegetables we eat. Amid the acres of almond trees and vineyards full of grapes live about four million people, a population roughly the size of Connecticut's.

Many middle-class families saw a life in Fresno as their best shot at the American Dream. It was a place with promise, a place where they could afford a real single-family home on a nice, quiet street, with a good school nearby for their kids.

Not big-city and not country either, new suburban developments seemed to sprout up every month, taking root in the fertile soil as if they were another crop.

Around two decades ago banks started making lots of home loans in places like Fresno. The idea of giving more people a shot at owning their own home sounds nice, but there was a dark side, too.

Say a home costs $200,000. A borrower has to pay back that loan plus interest, a small percent of the loan, on top of the actual loan. Interest is kind of like paying for the privilege to have access to all of that money. And it all works out when people have steady jobs and can pay the money back, or when the interest rate stays roughly the same for the life of the loan. But when home-buying in places like Fresno started to explode, bankers didn't stick to those rules.

Lenders at banks became more and more aggressive, luring borrowers with exciting loan offers that made it all seem so easy. Banks were offering loans to people who couldn't possibly pay them back—people with no jobs at all or jobs that paid very little. And if the banks' offers seemed too good to be true, it's because they were. Loans might start out with a low interest rate, but after a few months of really low payments, the interest rates on them would spike very high and people wouldn't be able to afford them. These loans were called subprime or adjustable-rate mortgages. People would open the mail and find a bill that they simply could not afford to pay. In many of those cases, the bank would foreclose on a home—literally taking people's homes away from them.

This wasn't just happening in Fresno. This was happening all over the country, to millions of American families. But why? Why would banks lend to people who couldn't pay them back? There are a bunch of reasons. For one thing, if the loan went sour, at the very least, the bank would own the home through foreclosure. But the real reasons lie deeper in our complex financial system, of which mortgage lenders are just one piece. Lots of powerful people bent the rules and built elaborate schemes to make money off these bad loans. Even though most Americans didn't realize it, our entire economy had grown dependent on these scams. But it was like building a tower of blocks on top of a balloon, and when the balloon popped, the entire economy came crashing down, and we ended up with the Great Recession.

This happened in every part of America. Consider the story of Karina and Juan Santillan, who bought a home twenty miles east of Los Angeles in 1999. After a few years they were persuaded to take out an adjustable-rate mortgage on their home. At the time, their monthly payment was $1,200. By 2009 it had jumped to $3,000—and Karina had lost her job. Suddenly at risk of losing their house, they contacted a company that promised to protect them. After paying $6,800 for services that were supposed to help, they realized they had been scammed. Ten years after purchasing their home, they were forced to tell their four children they were going to have to leave.

This pattern played out with particular force in Fresno and Stockton. Local leaders pleaded with the federal government to declare the region a disaster area, like after a flood or a hurricane, and send help. "Disaster area" was a suitable description: entire neighborhoods were abandoned, and the area was suffering one of the highest foreclosure rates in the nation. Sometimes families were struggling so hard to pay their mortgages that they would abruptly pick up and leave. There were reports of pets being abandoned because their owners could no longer afford to keep them. When I visited Fresno, I was told that abandoned dogs had been seen roaming in packs. I felt like I was walking through the aftermath of a natural disaster. But this disaster was man-made.

When the crash finally bottomed out, 8.4 million Americans nationwide had lost their jobs. Roughly 5 million homeowners were at least two months behind on their mortgages. And 2.5 million foreclosure proceedings had begun.

But foreclosure is not just a statistic.

Foreclosure is a dad suffering in silence, knowing he's in trouble but too ashamed to tell his family that he has failed. Foreclosure is a mother on the phone with her bank, pleading for more time—just until the school year is over. Foreclosure is the sheriff knocking at your door and ordering you out of your home. It is a grandmother on the sidewalk in tears, watching her life's belongings being removed from her house by strangers and left exposed in the yard. It is learning from a neighbor that your house was just auctioned off on the steps of City Hall. It is the changing of locks, the death of dreams. It is a child learning for the first time that parents can be terrified, too.

Homeowners told me countless stories of personal disaster. And as the months dragged on, we learned about sketchy practices in the foreclosure process. There were stories of homeowners learning that their bank couldn't find their mortgage documents. There were stories of people discovering that they actually owed tens of thousands of dollars less than the banks said they did. A man in Florida had his house foreclosed on and put up for sale—even though he'd bought the house with cash and never had a mortgage.

There were stories of banks foreclosing on homes even after working out new, modified payment plans with homeowners. The banks left homeowners with no explanation, no point of contact, and no options.

Clearly, something had gone wrong. But it wasn't until the end of September 2010 that a major part of the scandal would break wide open. That was when we learned that the country's largest banks—including Bank of America, JPMorgan Chase, and Wells Fargo—had been illegally foreclosing on people's homes since 2007, using a practice that became known as "robo-signing."

We learned that to speed up the foreclosure process,

financial institutions hired "foreclosure experts" who weren't experts at all. Often they were people with no formal financial training—from Walmart floor workers to hair stylists—who were placed in positions with one responsibility: sign off on foreclosures by the thousands.

Robo-signers admitted that they didn't really understand the documents they were paid to approve. The job was simply to sign their name, or to forge someone else's. They got paid $10 an hour. And they got bonuses for volume—the more foreclosures they signed, the more money they got. The banks that engineered these schemes didn't care that they were breaking the law and hurting people.

On October 13, 2010, the attorneys general of all fifty states agreed to join together in what's known as a multistate investigation. It was billed as a comprehensive, nationwide law enforcement effort to uncover the banks' actions in the foreclosure crisis.

I was eager to join the fight, but there was just one small problem: I wasn't yet California's attorney general.

I was in the middle of my campaign for that office when the investigation was announced, and there were still three weeks left until Election Day. The polls were predicting a very close race.

* * *

On Election Night 2010, I lost the race for attorney general. Three weeks later, I won.

I'd started the evening with what had become a ritual: a friends-and-family dinner, followed by the Election Night party. We arrived as results started to trickle in from around the state. In the main room, supporters were gathered waiting in anticipation for the results. Behind them stood risers for TV cameras and reporters facing the stage. We went in through the back and into a side room where my staff was gathered. They had arranged four tables into a square, and most of them were sitting there, staring at their laptops, hitting *refresh* on the websites keeping track of the vote tally. I greeted everyone, my spirits high, and thanked them for all their hard work.

Then Ace Smith, my chief strategist, pulled me aside. "How's it looking?" I asked.

"It's going to be a very long night," Ace said. My opponent was in the lead.

I'd always known that I could take nothing for granted. Even plenty of fellow Democrats had considered me a long shot, and some hadn't held back in saying so. One longtime political strategist announced to an audience that there was no way I could win, because I was "a woman running for attorney general, a woman who is a minority, a woman who is a minority who is anti–death penalty, a woman who is a minority who is anti–death penalty who is DA of wacky San Francisco." Old stereotypes die hard. I was convinced that my perspective and experience made me the strongest candidate in the race, but I didn't know if the voters would agree. The past few weeks, I'd done so much knocking on wood—and knocking on voters' doors—that my knuckles were bruised.

By 10 p.m., we were not much closer to knowing the outcome of the race. I was trailing, but we knew that a lot of voting sites had yet to report. Ace suggested that I go out and address the crowd. "The TV cameras aren't going to stay much longer," he said, "so if you have a message for your supporters tonight, I think you should do that now." It sounded like a smart idea to me.

I left the staff room, spent a few quiet minutes thinking about what I would say, then straightened my suit jacket and walked into the main room and onto the stage. I told the audience that it was going to be a long night, but that it was going to be a good night, too. My opponent was losing ground by the minute, I assured them. I reminded them what our campaign was about and what we stood for. "This campaign is so much bigger than me. It is so much bigger than any one person."

At some point during my speech, I noticed a shift in the room. People seemed to be getting emotional. I was just finishing my remarks when I saw Debbie Mesloh, my longtime communications adviser, approaching. She mouthed to me, "Get off the stage and go to the back room, now." That wasn't reassuring. I finished my remarks and was making my way to Debbie when I was stopped by a reporter and her cameraman.

"So what do you think happened?" she asked, putting the microphone in my face.

"I think we ran a really great race and it's going to be a long night," I said.

The reporter seemed confused, and so was I. The more questions she asked, the more it was clear we weren't connecting at all. Clearly something had happened, and I was out of the loop. When I finally got back to the staff room, I learned what. While I'd been onstage, talking about what lay ahead, the *San Francisco Chronicle* newspaper had called the race for my opponent. No wonder people were crying! I'd been the only one out there who thought we were still in the game.

Realizing that our hometown paper had called the race against us felt like a punch in the gut. The mood was grim as my team and I huddled together in the back room. After so many months of working so hard, excitement was giving way to exhaustion. I looked around at the slumping shoulders and sad expressions. I couldn't bear the thought of sending our volunteers home feeling this way.

Ace called me over. "Listen, I'm looking at the numbers, and a lot of our strongest areas haven't come in. They called the race too early. We're still in this."

I knew he couldn't see the future—but Ace wasn't the kind of person who told soothing lies just to make me feel better. He knew every precinct, every voting site in California better than perhaps anyone in the state. If he thought we were still in it, I believed him. I told my supporters we weren't giving up.

My opponent had a different view of things. Around 11 p.m., he stood up in front of the cameras and delivered a speech in Los Angeles declaring victory. But we waited. And waited—getting regular updates from the field and trying to keep one another's spirits high.

Around 1 a.m., I leaned over to my childhood friend Derreck, who owned a chicken and waffle restaurant in Oakland. "Is your kitchen still open?"

"Don't worry," he promised. "I'll take care of it."

Sure enough, the next thing I knew, the room was filled

with the mouthwatering aroma of fried chicken and corn bread and greens and candied yams. We all gathered around the aluminum pans and ate. About an hour later, with 89 percent of the precincts in, we were tied.

Finally, I turned to Maya. "I'm exhausted. Do you think anybody's going to have a problem if I leave?"

"Everybody will be fine," she assured me. "People are waiting for you to leave so they can, too."

The next morning I learned that more votes had come in, and I was now ahead in the race, albeit only by a few thousand votes. With two million votes still waiting to be tallied, there was a good chance we weren't going to know the results for weeks. And so we sent out teams to monitor the vote counts and we waited. We realized that nothing was likely to happen with the count over Thanksgiving weekend, so we sent everyone home to be with their families. Early Wednesday morning, I headed for the airport to catch a flight to New York. I was going to spend the holiday with Maya, my brother-in-law, Tony, and my niece, Meena.

As my cab was pulling off the highway, I got a text from a district attorney who had supported my opponent. "I look forward to working with you," it read. Again, someone else knew more information than I did. Had something else happened with the recount? Once I got on the plane and settled into my seat I noticed that I'd missed an incoming call when I had gone through airport security. There was a voicemail from my opponent asking me to call him back. I dialed his number as the cabin doors were closing and the flight attendants were directing passengers to put their cell phones away.

"I want you to know I'll be conceding," he said. I couldn't believe it! He had looked at the numbers and realized he had no chance of beating me now. I was going to be the Attorney General of California.

"You ran a great race," I said.

"I hope you know how big a job this is going to be," he added.

"Have a nice Thanksgiving with your family," I replied.

And that was it. Of the nearly nine million ballots cast statewide, I had won by the equivalent of three votes per precinct. I was so relieved, so excited, so ready to start. I wanted to call everyone, but the next thing I knew, we were barreling down the runway, and then we were in the air—with no Wi-Fi. My twenty-one-day Election Night was over, and all I could do was sit there. Alone with my thoughts. For five hours.

✶ ✶ ✶

Because the count had taken so long, there was only a month to process the victory before my swearing-in. And beyond the election, I was also still processing the grief of my mother's death. She'd passed away almost two years before, in February 2009, as the long, hard-fought campaign was just getting under way. It was crushing to lose her. I knew what my election would have meant to her. How I wished she could be there to see it and celebrate with me.

When January 3, 2011, arrived, I walked down the stairs of the California Museum for Women, History, and the Arts, in Sacramento, to greet the standing-room-only crowd. Flags were waving, dignitaries were there, observers peered down from the balcony. Maya held Mrs. Shelton's Bible as I took the oath of office. But what I remember most vividly about the day was the worry I felt about saying my mother's name in my speech without crying. I'd practiced over and over again, and choked up every time. But it was important to me that her name be spoken in that room, because none of what I had achieved would have been possible without her.

"Today, with this oath," I told the crowd, "we affirm the principle that every Californian matters."

It was a principle that would be put to the test in the weeks that followed. Later that month, 37,000 homeowners lined up in Los Angeles to plead with banks to modify their mortgages so they could stay in their homes.

On my first day in office, I gathered my senior team and told them that we needed to get involved right away in the multistate investigation into the banks. Inside the office we were preparing for battle. Outside the office, we were constantly reminded of who we were fighting for. At every public event we held, there was always a group of people—sometimes five or ten or twenty—who had come in the hope of seeing me and asking for my help, face-to-face. Most brought their paperwork with them—folders and envelopes overflowing with mortgage documents and foreclosure notices and handwritten notes. Some had driven hundreds of miles to find me.

I'll never forget the woman who interrupted a small health care event I was doing at Stanford. She stood up in the audience, tears streaming down her face, desperation in her voice. "I need help. You need to help me. I need you to help call the bank and tell them to let me stay in my home. Please, I'm begging you." It was heartbreaking.

I also knew there were tens of thousands of people just like her, fighting for their lives, who didn't have the ability to track down the attorney general in person. So we went directly to them, holding meetings in community centers across the state.

I wanted them to see us. I also wanted my team to see them, so that when they were sitting across from the bank executives in a conference room, they'd remember who they were representing. At one of these gatherings, I was speaking to a man about the problems he was having with the banks. His young son was playing quietly nearby. And then the little boy came over and looked up at his father.

"Daddy, what does 'underwater' mean?"

I could see the awful fear in his eyes. He thought his father was literally drowning. Even though it might have felt like that, what it really meant was that his father owed more money to the bank on his house than his house would be worth if he sold it. So he could end up without a house, but still be in debt to the bank.

Either way, it was a terrible thing to consider. But the metaphor made sense: a lot of people had gone under. Still more were clinging by their fingernails to the edge. And every day that went by, more and more of those desperate people were losing their grip.

At one homeowners' meeting, a woman described with pride the home she had saved up to buy in 1997—the first home she'd ever purchased as an adult. After falling one month behind on a loan payment in early 2009, she'd called her lender asking for advice. Representatives for the lender said they could help, but after months of their insisting she produce and send them endless paperwork, of sending her documents without explanation and demanding that she sign, of keeping her in the dark as she sought answers to her questions, her home was foreclosed upon from under her feet.

Fighting back tears as she shared her story with me, she said, "I'm sorry. I know it's just a house . . ." But she knew, as we all do, that it's never "just a house."

My first opportunity to get personally involved in the multistate talks arrived in early March. The National Association of Attorneys General was holding its annual multiday meeting at the Fairmont hotel, in Washington, DC. I flew in with my team. All fifty attorneys general were there from every state, seated in alphabetical order by state. I took my spot between Arkansas and Colorado.

As the conversation turned from general business to the multistate investigation, it suddenly became clear to me that the investigation wasn't complete; there were still many unanswered questions. But they were ready to allow the banks to settle out of court. The banks could pay some money, which the states would divvy up, and then never have to worry about being sued.

I was stunned. How did they come up with the sum they were going to agree to? What was the dollar amount based on? How could we negotiate a settlement when we hadn't completed an investigation?

But what shocked me most wasn't the choosing of an arbitrary dollar figure. It was that in exchange for settling, the banks could never be sued in the future for whatever crimes they might have committed during that time period. This was insane. We hadn't even finished the investigation, so we didn't know what crimes we might uncover!

During a break in the session, I gathered my team. The settlement was going to be on the agenda again in the afternoon.

"I'm not going to that meeting," I told them. "This thing is baked." California had more foreclosures than any other state, which meant lots more people had the potential to sue the banks for lots more money in California. We had power in numbers. If the banks couldn't get a settlement with me—representing the people of California—they weren't going to settle with anyone. It was one thing to know I had this power; it was another to convince the others I was willing to use it. If I skipped the afternoon session, my empty chair would express that message better than I ever could.

My staff and I left the Fairmont and took a cab to the

Justice Department. We called Tom Perrelli on the way, to let him know we were coming. It was his job, among other things, to oversee the multistate investigation on behalf of the federal government. I told him that of the ten cities hit hardest by the foreclosure crisis at the time, seven were in California; that it was my job to get to the bottom of it; and that I couldn't sign on to anything that was going to keep me from doing my own investigation.

Perrelli made the case that my investigation wouldn't turn up what I hoped it would, that going after the big banks was not something any one state could do, even the biggest state in the nation. And, he added, whatever I'd try would take years. By the time I got what California deserved, the people who needed help would have already lost their homes. This was the reason there hadn't been a thorough investigation; there simply wasn't time. I didn't agree with him.

We flew home that night and got right to work. I had been told that, as things stood, California was going to get somewhere between $2 billion and $4 billion in the settlement. Some of the lawyers in the office thought it was a big number, big enough to take. My point to them was: Compared with what? That kind of money could purchase a handful of airplanes, but could it make the homeowners of California whole?

A report showed that in the course of about five years an average of five hundred California families had lost their homes each day. If the banks' illegal scheme had caused a lot more than $2 billion to $4 billion in damage, then those really big numbers would start to look really small.

After experts reviewed the figures, I found out that the results were as unacceptable as I had feared. Compared with the devastation, the banks were offering us crumbs, nowhere near enough to compensate for the damage they had caused.

"We need to be prepared to walk away from the settlement," I told my team. "There's no way I'm taking this offer." I told them that it was time to open up our own independent investigation.

The fact that we were doing our own investigation angered the multistate negotiators. The banks were furious that I was causing trouble. The settlement was now in doubt. But this had been my goal.

In this situation, the harm was still unfolding. While negotiations went on, hundreds of thousands more homeowners had gotten notices that they would lose their homes. It was happening every day and in real time. There were huge areas, entire zip codes, where people were hundreds of thousands of dollars underwater. My team and I pored over the numbers weekly—a dashboard of despair, describing how many people were thirty, sixty, ninety days from losing their homes.

Before I walked away from the negotiations, I wanted to take one last shot at getting a fair deal and some real relief for my state.

The next meeting was being held in September, and the lawyers of the major banks had asked me to attend. I was sure they wanted me there so they could size me up from across the table—this new attorney general from out of nowhere. Good. I wanted to size them up, too.

We arrived at the offices of Debevoise & Plimpton, the Washington law firm that was hosting the meeting. We were led into a large conference room where more than a dozen people were gathered.

After a few polite hellos, we took our seats around a long, imposing conference table. I sat at one head of the table. The chief attorneys of the big banks were there, along with a fleet of Wall Street's best lawyers.

The meeting was tense from the moment it began. Bank of America's lawyer opened by turning to my negotiating team and complaining about the terrible pain we were putting the banks through. I'm not kidding. She said that the process was frustrating, that the bank had been through enormous trauma, that employees there were working to respond to all the investigations and changes to rules and practices since the crash. Everyone was exhausted, she told us. And she wanted answers from California. What was the holdup?

I ripped right in. "You want to talk about pain? Do you have any understanding of the pain that you've caused?" I felt it in my bones. It made me so angry to see these guys dismiss the suffering of homeowners. "There are a million children in California who aren't going to be able to go to their school anymore because their parents lost their home. If you want to talk about pain, I'll tell you about some pain."

The bank representatives were calm but defensive. They said the homeowners were to blame for getting into mortgages they couldn't afford. I wasn't having any of that. I kept thinking about what the home-buying process looks like in real life.

For most families, buying a home is the biggest purchase they will ever make. It's a really special moment in your life, proof of all your hard work. You trust the people involved in the process. When the banker tells you that you qualify for a loan, you trust that she's reviewed the numbers and won't let you take on more than you can handle. When it comes time to finish the paperwork, it's basically a signing ceremony that feels like a celebration. When the bankers put a stack of paper in front of you, you trust them, and you sign. And sign. And sign. And sign.

I surveyed the roomful of lawyers, and I was certain that not one of them had read every word of their own mortgage documents before buying their first house. When I bought my apartment, I didn't.

The bankers spoke about mortgages seemingly without any sense of what they represented to the people involved, or who those people were. They seemed to be judging the character and values of struggling homeowners. I'd met many of those people. And for them, buying a home was more than an investment of money. I thought about Mr. Shelton, who was always in the front yard, pruning his roses in the morning, always mowing or watering or fertilizing. At one point, I asked one of the lawyers, "Haven't you ever known somebody who was proud of their lawn?"

The back-and-forth continued. They seemed to be under the wrong impression that I could be bullied into giving up. I wasn't budging. Toward the end of the meeting, the lead lawyer of JPMorgan chimed in with what he thought was a smart tactic. He told me that his parents were from California and that they had voted for me and liked me. And he knew there were a lot of voters back home who would be really happy with me if I just settled. It was great politics—he was sure of it.

I looked him straight in the eye: "Do I need to remind you this is a law enforcement action?" The room went quiet. After forty-five minutes, the conversation had gone on long enough.

"Look, your offer doesn't come near acknowledging the damage you have caused," I told them. "And you should know that I mean what I say. I'm going to investigate everything. Everything."

The general counsel of Wells Fargo turned to me.

"Well, if you're going to keep investigating, why should we settle with you?"

"You have to make that decision for yourself," I told him.

After I left the meeting, I announced my decision to pull out of the negotiations altogether.

I started getting phone calls. From friends who were afraid that I had made too powerful an enemy. From political consultants who warned me to brace myself because the banks were going to spend tens of millions of dollars to throw me out of office. From the governor of California: "I hope you know what you're doing." From White House officials and cabinet secretaries, trying to bring me back to the talks. The pressure was intense—and constant—and it was coming from all sides: from longtime supporters and longtime opponents and everyone in between.

But there was another kind of pressure, too. Millions of homeowners had raised their voices, along with activists and advocacy organizations that were mobilizing based on our strategy. We knew we weren't alone.

Still, this period was hard. We'd refused that $2 to $4 billion, without knowing if we'd get anything at all. Before bed, I would say a small prayer: "God, please help me do the right thing." I'd pray that I was choosing the right path, and for the courage to stay the course. Most of all, I'd pray that the families counting on me remained safe and secure. I knew how much was at stake.

I often found myself thinking about my mother and what she would have done. I know she would have told me to hold on to my beliefs; to listen to my gut. Tough decisions are tough precisely because the outcome isn't clear. But your gut—guided by your values—will tell you if you're on the right track. And you'll know what decision to make.

By January, the banks were frustrated and furious, feeling that we had pushed too far.

I pulled my team into my office and we tried to figure out a next step—if there was one to be taken. Had we killed the possibility of any deal? Was there still a chance? I needed to be sure. We sat in silence for a while, thinking it through, until an idea popped into my head. I shouted for my assistant next door. "Get me Jamie Dimon on the phone." Dimon was and—as of this writing—remains the chairman and CEO of JPMorgan Chase, one of the biggest banks in the country.

About ten seconds later, my assistant popped her head into my office. "Mr. Dimon is on the line." I picked up the receiver.

"You're trying to steal from my shareholders!" he yelled, almost as soon as he heard my voice.

I gave it right back. "*Your* shareholders? *Your* shareholders? *My* shareholders are the homeowners of California! You come and see them. Talk to them about who got robbed." It stayed at that level for a while. We were like dogs in a fight. A member of my senior team later recalled thinking, "This was either a really good or a colossally bad idea."

I'll never know what happened on Dimon's side. But I do know that two weeks later, the banks gave in. When all was said and done, instead of the $2 billion to $4 billion that was originally on the table, we secured an $18 billion deal, which ultimately grew to $20 billion in relief to homeowners. It was a tremendous victory for the people of California.

I had been asked to fly to Washington to be part of the larger announcement, a major press conference and celebration that would take place at the Department of Justice and the White House. But I wanted to be at home with my team. It was our victory to share together. And we needed to gear up for the battles ahead.

Four

WEDDING BELLS

Whenever I travel to a country for the first time, I try to visit the highest court in the land. They are monuments of a certain kind, built not just to house a courtroom but to send a message. In New Delhi, for example, the Supreme Court of India is designed to symbolize the balancing scales of justice. In Jerusalem, Israel's iconic Supreme Court building combines straight lines—which represent the rigid nature of the law—with curved walls and glass that represent the fluid nature of justice. These are buildings that speak.

The same can be said of the United States Supreme Court Building, which, to my mind, is the most beautiful of them all. Its architecture recalls ancient Greece and the earliest days of democracy, as though you are standing in front of a modern-day Parthenon. It is grand and commanding while also dignified and restrained. As you walk up the steps toward an extraordinary entryway of Corinthian columns, you can see our nation's founding hopes in its architecture. It is there that the words EQUAL JUSTICE UNDER LAW are engraved in stone. And it was that promise that brought me to the Supreme Court Building on March 26, 2013.

I arrived and was escorted to my seat in the courtroom. Because the Supreme Court justices don't allow photography or video inside, this is a place that most of the country never sees. I certainly hadn't before that day. I gazed around in awe: the stunning pink marble; the vivid red draping and intricate ceiling; the imposing bench with its nine empty chairs. I kept thinking about all the history that had been made inside these walls. But unlike a museum or a war memorial, where history is preserved for future generations, the Supreme Court is a place where history is active and alive, where it continues to unfold with every decision.

A little after 10 a.m., we rose as the nine justices entered the courtroom and took their seats.

"We'll hear argument this morning in Case 12-144, *Hollingsworth v. Perry*," said Chief Justice John Roberts.

Back in 2008, California's voters approved a measure called Proposition 8, outlawing marriages for same-sex couples in the state. Most elections are held to choose between candidates to lead an office of government, like governor, attorney general, senator, or president. Those elected officials then set government policy. Ballot initiatives like Prop 8, as it was known, are ways for voters in certain states to make policy directly, without the elected officials as the middlemen. But Prop 8 discriminated against people based on their sexual orientation. It was wrongheaded and seemed to be unconstitutional, too. Its day in court had been a long time coming.

But that's not where all this started. In the year 2000, eight years before Prop 8, California voters approved a ballot initiative—Prop 22 (also known as the Knight Initiative, after its author, state senator William "Pete" Knight)—that required the state to define marriage as a union between people of the opposite sex—a man and a woman. For years we fought it—in the streets, at the ballot box, and in the courts. Even my then–school-aged niece, Meena, got in on the action; I remember, one time, going to pick her up at her high school and being told she was in a student meeting. When I got to the classroom, young Meena was in front, rallying the other kids: "This isn't a Knight Initiative—it's a nightmare!"

During Valentine's Day week in 2004, then–San Francisco mayor Gavin Newsom decided to ignore Prop 22 and allow marriages for same-sex couples anyway.

When I was passing by San Francisco City Hall, I saw

throngs of people lined up around the block, waiting to get in. They were counting down the minutes before the California government would finally recognize their right to marry whomever they loved. You could feel the joy and anticipation in the air. Some of these couples had been waiting decades.

It was such an extraordinary sight that I got out of my car and walked up the steps of City Hall, where I bumped into a city official. "Kamala, come and help us," she said, a glowing smile on her face. "We need more people to perform the marriages." I was delighted to be a part of it.

I was quickly sworn in, along with numerous city officials. We stood together performing marriages in the hallway, crowded into every nook and cranny of City Hall. There was all this wonderful excitement building as we welcomed the waves of loving couples, one by one, to be married then and there. It was unlike anything I had ever been a part of before. And it was beautiful.

But not long after, the marriages were invalidated. The couples who had been so happy and hopeful received letters telling them that their marriage licenses would not be recognized under the law. It was, for each and every one of them, a devastating setback.

In May 2008, the California Supreme Court came to the

rescue. As the highest court in California, its role is similar to the U.S. Supreme Court. Its decisions on California law are the final word for state legal battles, whereas the U.S. Supreme Court provides the last word on national or federal legal issues. The court held that the same-sex marriage ban was unconstitutional, which paved the way for lesbian, gay, bisexual, transgender, and queer (LGBTQ) couples to realize the equal dignity they had always deserved, regardless of their gender identity or sexual orientation. And over the next six months, eighteen thousand same-sex couples exchanged wedding vows in California.

But in November 2008, on the same night that Barack Obama was elected president, the people of California narrowly voted to pass Prop 8, an amendment to the California Constitution that stripped same-sex couples of their right to marry. Because this was an amendment to the state's constitution, it couldn't be overturned by the legislature—the equivalent of the state's Congress—or the state court system. No new marriages could be performed. Couples who had already been married were placed in a cruel limbo.

There was one clear route left to justice: the federal courts. The American Foundation for Equal Rights, then led by Chad Griffin, filed a lawsuit on behalf of two same-sex couples—Kris

Perry and Sandy Stier; Paul Katami and Jeff Zarrillo—whose job was to represent in court the millions of people just like them, people who simply wanted the human dignity of marrying the person they loved and who deserved equal protection under the law.

It would take eight months for the lawsuit to make its way to the first stage of the fight: the U.S. federal district court. Inside that courtroom, a judge would hear from witnesses, review evidence, and, based on the facts before him, decide whether Prop 8 had violated the civil rights of Kris, Sandy, Jeff, and Paul. On August 4, 2010, Chief Judge Vaughn Walker ruled in their favor, concluding that Prop 8 was indeed unconstitutional and affirming the right of same-sex couples to marry. It was fantastic and important news. But, as is common practice, the judge decided he was going to wait to enforce the ruling—a legal concept known as a stay—until it was appealed to a higher court, which he knew was going to happen. And of course Prop 8 backers appealed, hoping that they'd win a ruling to outlaw same-sex marriage once and for all.

It took more than a year before the Ninth Circuit Court of Appeals issued its decision. Each day of delay represented justice denied—and much, much more. Each day of delay was a day a devoted couple couldn't marry. Each day of delay was a day a grandmother passed away before the wedding she would have loved to see. Each day of delay was a day a child was left wondering "Why can't my parents get married, too?"

The Appeals Court agreed with the lower court's ruling, which was great news, but proponents of Prop 8 kept going, all the way to the U.S. Supreme Court. The big issue was "standing." You don't get to be a party in a lawsuit simply because you have strong feelings about something. In order to bring a case in court, you are required to have standing, which means, among other things, that you have suffered or might suffer an actual injury.

Kris Perry had standing to sue the state when Prop 8 passed because it injured her; it stripped her of a civil right—the right to marry the woman she loved. Prop 8 treated one group of Americans differently from all other Americans, and that was unfair. Supporters of Prop 8 tried arguing that they were being harmed by the existence of same-sex marriages, but the courts wouldn't have it. When Prop 8 was thrown out in federal court, that decision gave protections to one group without taking away anything from anyone. The courts were saying: you can't take away people's rights because you don't like the notion of them having the same rights as you. Opponents of same-sex marriage would always have their freedom of expression. They could say and believe whatever they wanted. But they did not have the power to deny other Americans their right to marry.

As I left the Supreme Court, there were hundreds of people gathered, waving rainbow flags, holding signs, waiting anxiously for justice. It made me smile. They were why I had become a lawyer in the first place. It was in the courtroom, I believed, that you could translate that passion into action and law.

I looked out at their faces and imagined all the people who had stood in the same place for similar reasons: black parents with their children, fighting against segregation in schools; young women marching and shouting for the right to control their own bodies and end a pregnancy through legal abortion; civil rights activists demonstrating for full voting rights.

In everyday life, these activists over the years might have seemed like they had nothing in common. But on these steps, they shared something profound: in one form or another, they had faced treatment "directly subversive of the principle of equality," as Supreme Court Chief Justice Earl Warren had once put it.

And in one way or another, they believed the Constitution could set them free. They believed in the promise of that document, in the words of Franklin Roosevelt, "not because it is old but because it is ever new, not in the worship of its past alone but in the faith of the living who keep it young, now and in the years to come." So they marched. And they fought. And they waited.

I knew that nothing was certain. The Supreme Court had made some terrible decisions in its past. In 1889, it upheld a law—still not overturned—that specifically excluded Chinese people from immigrating to America. In 1896, it held that racial segregation did not violate the Constitution. In 1944, it held that there was nothing unconstitutional about forcing Japanese Americans into internment camps during World War II. In 1986, it held that gay relationships could be criminalized. And on the day before we would hear the ruling in our case, the Court's conservative justices invalidated—and gutted—a critical part of the Voting Rights Act, which had, since 1965, eliminated obstacles to voting. Nothing was certain.

But on the morning of June 26, 2013, we received wonderful news. The Supreme Court agreed that Prop 8 proponents had no standing to appeal, and dismissed the case in a 5–4 decision. That meant the lower court ruling would stand. And that meant marriage equality was the law again in California—finally.

I was in my office when the word came through. A

spontaneous celebration broke out, with whoops and applause ricocheting through the hallways. After so many years of struggle and setback, love had finally conquered all.

A few days later, my phone rang, and it was Chad Griffin. He was with Kris Perry and Sandy Stier.

"Kamala, we're coming to San Francisco. Sandy and Kris are going to be the first marriage, and we want you to perform the ceremony."

"Of course! I would love to!" I told Chad. "Nothing would make me more proud."

Normally, I had to travel by official car, but this time I insisted that we walk. As my team and I made our way to City Hall, I recalled the famous image of Thurgood Marshall striding purposefully with Autherine Lucy, who had been denied admission to the University of Alabama, one of the first tests of integration. Though we were the only ones in the street this time, it felt like we were leading our part of a parade—one that stretched through generations. We were following in the footsteps of giants, and widening the trail for our time.

When we reached City Hall, we made our way to the clerk's office, where a crowd was already gathering in the hallway. Kris and Sandy arrived soon after, beaming and ready to go.

This is me contemplating the future.

This is me with my father when I was 9 months old.

Here I am with my mother at 2 months old.

When I was 10 months old, I visited Jamaica. This is me with my mother and my grandfather on my dad's side.

Me and Maya on a walk with our mom in Madison, Wisconsin.

Maya and I loved Christmas. I'm 4 in this picture, and she's 2.

This is me with my cousins in Jamaica.

This is me eating an ice cone in Harlem, where I was visiting my uncle Freddy.

This is me at about 8, at my mom's lab. She would often take me to work with her on weekends or after school.

Maya and I loved dancing—and still do.

My grandparents on my mom's side came to visit us when I was 8.

This is me at 12.

I always loved riding on carousels.

My friends and me at law school graduation.

My husband, Doug, and me at the ballpark.

At my law school graduation with my first grade teacher, Mrs. Wilson, and my mom.

Me with Mrs. Shelton in her kitchen.

Me getting sworn in to my second term as the attorney general of California. Doug is holding the Bible.

Me in front of the Kamoji bus during my Senate race.

Election night in the U.S. Senate race.

Me and my mom at the Chinese New Year parade. She went to a lot of events with me.

I was honored to give a speech to students at Howard University.

"Congratulations!" I exclaimed as I hugged them both. They had been through so much, for so long. We were laughing and chatting.

Meanwhile, news started to spread, and people started coming to City Hall by the hundreds. Some to celebrate. Some to get married. Some just to bear witness. We could hear the Gay Men's Chorus singing, their voices soaring in the rotunda. As we filed into that confined space together, everyone experiencing pure joy, the feeling was magical.

We were preparing for the ceremony when somebody pulled me aside to say that the clerk in Los Angeles was refusing to issue marriage licenses until he heard from the state. He clearly needed direction. It was as simple as passing me the phone.

"This is Kamala Harris," I said. "You must start the marriages immediately."

"All right!" he responded, sounding relieved. "I will take that as our notice and we will issue the license now."

I thanked him. "And enjoy it!" I added. "It's going to be fun."

A short time later, I took my spot on the balcony and watched Kris and Sandy, followed by their loved ones and friends, walk up the stairs of City Hall. They made an elegant pair, in matching beige and white. Sandy was holding a bouquet of white roses. Two days earlier, they had become living symbols of justice. Now, as they took their final steps toward me, I could feel history being made.

"Today we witness not only the joining of Kris and Sandy, but the realization of their dream—marriage. . . . By joining the case against Proposition 8, they represented thousands of couples like themselves in the fight for marriage equality. Through the ups and downs, the struggles and the triumphs, they came out victorious."

Kris and Sandy exchanged their vows, and their son, Elliott, handed over the rings. I had the honor and privilege to say, "By virtue of the power and authority vested in me by the state of California, I now declare you spouses for life."

There were hundreds of weddings that day, all across the state, each one of them an expression of love and justice and hope. San Francisco City Hall was lit in the colors of the rainbow—a beautiful tribute to the beautiful words "I do!"

When I got home that evening, I had a chance to reflect on the day. My thoughts turned to a man I wished could have been there to see it. Jim Rivaldo, my friend and one of my most important advisers. He was a political strategist, an activist, and a leader of San Francisco's LGBTQ community. My family loved him, especially my mother. He spent Thanksgiving with us the year before he died, in 2007. My mother cared for him at his bedside, trying to keep him comfortable in his final days.

I wanted to talk to him. I wanted to share the moment with him. But even in his absence, I knew exactly what he would have said: *We're not done yet.*

It would take another two years before the Supreme Court recognized marriage equality in all fifty states. And today, it is still the case under federal law that an employer can fire an employee if they identify as LGBTQ. It is still the case, in statehouses across the country, that transgender rights—the rights of people who don't identify with the gender they were assigned at birth—are getting trampled. This is still very much an active civil rights battle.

What happened with Prop 8 was an important part of a longer journey, one that began before America was its own nation and one that will continue for decades to come. It is the story of people fighting for their humanity—for the simple idea that we should all be equal and free. It is the story of people fighting for the promise made to all future generations at the signing of the Declaration of Independence: that no government has the right to rob us of our life or our liberty or our humble pursuit of happiness.

In the years to come, what matters most is that we see ourselves in one another's struggles. Whether we are fighting for transgender rights or for an end to racial bias, whether we are fighting against housing discrimination or cruel immigration laws, no matter who we are or how we look or how little it may seem we have in common, the truth is, in the battle for civil rights and economic justice—equal opportunities to thrive and succeed—we are all the same. In the words of the great Bayard Rustin, organizer of the 1963 March on Washington for civil rights, "We are all one, and if we don't know it, we will learn it the hard way."

A few months after Kris and Sandy got married, I was on my way to an event at an organization called the California Endowment on a subject few might have expected to be on an attorney general's agenda. I was there to talk about elementary school truancy—when kids miss too many days of school— and to start a discussion about solutions.

When I first started as attorney general, I told my team that I wanted to make elementary school truancy a top priority for my office. Those who didn't know me must have thought I was joking. Why would the state's top law enforcement official want to focus on whether seven-year-olds are going to school or not? But those who had been with me for a while knew I wasn't messing around. Indeed, instituting a statewide plan on truancy was part of the reason I'd run for the office in the first place.

Back on Track, the program I created when I was district attorney, was all about helping young adults avoid prison time and all the bad outcomes that often flow from a felony conviction. But I was equally concerned about helping at-risk kids earlier, about the kinds of steps we could take as a community—and a country—to keep children safe and on track to begin with. I wanted to identify key moments in a child's life when my office could make a difference.

As I studied the research I started connecting the dots. The first dot concerned the importance of learning to read well by third grade. Up until that point, schools focus on teaching students to learn to read. In fourth grade, there's a shift, and students transition to reading in order to learn. If students can't read, they can't learn, and they fall further behind, month after month and year after year—which forces them onto a path to poverty that becomes harder and harder to escape. The door of opportunity closes on them when they're barely four feet tall. I believe it is practically a crime when a child goes without an education.

And then more dots. When we studied the data, we learned that, in San Francisco, more than 80 percent of prisoners were high school dropouts.

I went to see the school district superintendent, a wonderful woman named Arlene Ackerman, to ask her about the high school dropout rate. She told me that a big chunk of kids who skipped high school classes had also missed their elementary school classes—for weeks, even months at a time. That, to me, was a call to action.

The connections were so clear. You could map the path for children who started drifting away from the classroom when they were young. The truant child became the wanderer . . . who became the target for gangs looking for new recruits . . . who became the young drug seller . . . who became the perpetrator—or the victim—of violence. If we didn't see that child in elementary school, where they belonged, chances were we'd see them later in prison, in the hospital, or dead.

As we dug into the issue, we found that most parents have a natural desire to be good parents and help their kids stay in school. They want to be good fathers and mothers. They just may not have the skills or the money they need.

Imagine a single parent, working two low-wage shift jobs, six days a week, and still trapped below the poverty line. She gets paid by the hour and her job doesn't include benefits like getting paid during a vacation or for time she has to take off when she's sick. If her three-year-old daughter runs a fever, she can't bring her to the day care she took a second job to pay for, because other kids will get sick. There's no money for a babysitter, but if she stays home from work that day, she's not going to get paid, so she won't be able to afford diapers for the rest of the month. It's already been hard enough saving money to buy new shoes for her eleven-year-old son, whose feet seem to grow a whole size every few months.

What amounts to a headache for those with money to spare or some savings or a job that pays for sick leave takes the form of desperation for those without. If a parent in that situation asks her son to stay home from school for a day in order to take care of his little sister, we can't accuse her of loving her children any less. This is a matter of circumstance and condition, not of character. She wants to be the best parent she can.

The goal of our truancy prevention initiative was to step in and provide support. To show schools and parents that there were resources they could access to help their kids.

When I became attorney general, I wanted to use the power of my office to expose the truancy crisis across the state.

Our first report, the results of which I was announcing

that day at the California Endowment, estimated that we had approximately a million truant elementary school kids across the state. And in too many schools, nearly everyone was truant: one school had a truancy rate higher than 92 percent. Ninety-two out of every one hundred kids didn't come to school often enough!

While I was speaking, I noticed that two of my staffers were whispering to each other while pointing to a man in the audience. I couldn't hear them, but I knew exactly what they were saying: "Who's that guy? Is that him?" And I knew they were saying it because that guy was Doug.

Six months earlier, I hadn't known who that guy Doug was, either. I just knew that my best friend, Chrisette, was blowing up my phone. I was in the middle of a meeting, and my phone wouldn't stop buzzing. I ignored her call the first several times, but then I started to get worried. Her children are my godchildren. Had something happened?

I stepped out and called her.

"What's going on? Is everything okay?"

"Yes, everything is great. You're going on a date," she said.

"I am?"

"You are," she replied with total certainty. "I just met this guy. He's cute and he's the managing partner of his law firm and I think you're going to really like him. He's based in Los Angeles, but you're always here anyway."

Chrisette is like a sister to me, and I knew there was no use in arguing with her.

"What's his name?" I asked.

"His name is Doug Emhoff, but promise me you won't Google him. Don't overthink it. Just meet him. I already gave him your number. He's going to reach out."

Part of me groaned, but at the same time, I appreciated Chrisette's take-charge approach. She was one of the only people I talked to about my personal life. I was in the public eye, and I knew that single women in politics are viewed differently than single men. Reporters pay a lot of attention when they see us out on dates and write articles about it in their papers and on their websites. I had no interest in inviting that kind of scrutiny unless I was close to sure I'd found "the One"—which meant that for years, I kept my personal life separate from my career.

A few nights later, I was on my way to an event when I received a text from a number I didn't recognize. Doug was watching a basketball game with a friend, and he'd worked up the courage to send me an awkward text. "Hey! It's Doug. Just saying hi! I'm at the Lakers game." I wrote back to say hi, and we made plans to talk the following day. Then I punctuated it with my own bit of awkwardness—"Go Lakers!"—even though I'm really a Warriors fan.

The next morning, I was leaving the gym before work when I noticed that I had missed a call from Doug.

The voicemail, which I still have saved to this day, was long and a little rambling. He sounded like a nice guy, though, and I was intrigued to learn more. So I decided I'd give him a call.

He picked up, and we ended up on the phone for an entire hour. It sounds corny, I know, but the conversation just flowed; and even though I'm sure that both of us were trying extra hard to seem witty and interesting, most of all I remember us cracking each other up, joking and laughing at ourselves and with each other. We made dinner plans for Saturday night in Los Angeles. I could hardly wait.

Doug had been married once before, and he had two kids, Cole and Ella. When Doug and I first started dating, Ella was in middle school and Cole was in high school; Doug shared custody with his first wife, Kerstin. I had—and have—tremendous admiration and respect for Kerstin. I could tell from the way Doug talked about his kids that she was a terrific mother—and in later months, as Kerstin and I got to know each other, we really hit it off ourselves and became friends.

As a child of divorce, I knew how hard it can be when your parents start to date other people. So Doug and I put a lot of thought into when and how my first meeting with his kids should go. We waited until about two months after we'd met and by the time the big day finally arrived, I felt like I'd loved Doug for years.

I woke up that morning feeling incredibly excited, but also with some butterflies in my stomach. Until that moment, I'd known Cole and Ella as gorgeous faces in Doug's photographs, charming characters in his stories, the central figures in his heart. Now I was finally going to meet these two amazing young people. It was a momentous occasion.

On my way home from work, I picked up a tin of cookies and tied a festive ribbon around it. I got rid of my suit, changed into jeans and sneakers, took a few deep breaths, and got a ride to Doug's house. On the way over, I tried to imagine how the first few minutes would go. I ran scenarios in my head and tried to come up with the perfect things to say. The tin of cookies was sitting beside me on the seat, a silent witness to my rehearsing. Would the kids think the cookies were really nice or really weird? Maybe the ribbon was too much.

The ribbon was probably too much. But Cole and Ella could not have been more welcoming. They'd been wanting to meet me, too. We talked for a few minutes, then piled into Doug's car for dinner together. Doug and I had decided the kids should choose where we ate, to make everything as comfortable as possible. They'd picked a place that had been a favorite since they were younger—a seafood hut off the Pacific Coast Highway called the Reel Inn. It was about an hour away in traffic, which gave us some quality car time to get to know one another. Cole, it turned out, was a music aficionado, and he was excited to share some of his latest discoveries with me.

"I just started listening to Roy Ayers," he said. "Do you know him?"

I sang back: "Everybody loves the sunshine, sunshine, folks get down in the sunshine . . ."

"You know it!"

"Of course I know it!"

We put on the song, and then another and another. The four of us sang together with the windows rolled down as we drove up the coast to dinner.

The Reel Inn was casual and it was hard not to feel at ease. We sat at picnic tables with a view of the ocean, just as the sun was beginning to set. When we were done eating, Cole and Ella told us that they were going to head over to Cole's school to see an art show where some of their friends' work would be displayed. They wanted to know if we wanted to join them.

"Of course!" I said, as if this was a totally normal thing. It sounded great to me. Then Doug whispered to me, "They must like you. They never invite me to anything." We went to the school together, and Ella—a gifted artist—expertly guided us through the exhibit. Lots of their friends were there, too, and we had fun mingling and making conversation with the students and their parents. Doug later joked that I got completely overwhelmed with their lives that night, but I think it's more accurate to say that I was hooked, and Cole and Ella reeled me in.

At the end of March 2014, I had two trips planned. One was to Mexico for important work meetings. The other was to Italy, where Doug and I were looking forward to a romantic getaway. The night I got back from Mexico, I had to get ready for our Italy trip. Not the worst thing in the world by far, but I was frustrated: I'd had no time to pack and now I was panicking. Why? I couldn't find my black pants.

It was ridiculous, of course, but I had a hundred things racing through my mind and I was trying to shift gears for a getaway with my sweetheart. I was beating myself up for trying to do too much, even as I worried that I wasn't doing quite enough, and all of this stress gelled in the form of a search for my black pants.

Which I couldn't find. My closet was a mess.

I was frazzled, and when Doug arrived he seemed out of sorts as well. He was acting strange—a little stiff, a little quiet.

"Do you mind if we get takeout instead of going out to eat?" I asked him. "I didn't plan for this very well and I need time to pack."

"Of course," he said. "How about the Thai place we like?"

"Sounds great," I replied. I rifled through a kitchen drawer and produced a tattered paper menu. "How about pad thai?"

Doug turned to me. "I want to spend my life with you."

That was sweet, but he was always sweet like that. Truth be told, I didn't register the significance of what he'd said at all. I didn't even look up. My mind was still on the black pants.

"That's nice, honey," I said, rubbing his arm as I looked over the menu. "Should we have chicken or shrimp on the pad thai?"

"No, I want to spend my life with you," he said again. When I looked up, he was getting down on one knee. He'd concocted an elaborate plan to propose to me in Italy. But once he had the ring, it was burning a hole in his pocket. He couldn't keep it secret.

I looked at him there, on one knee, and burst into tears. Doug reached for my hand and I held my breath and smiled back. Then he asked me to marry him, and I bellowed a tear-soaked "Yes!"

Doug and I were married on Friday, August 22, 2014, in a small ceremony with the people we loved. Maya officiated; my niece, Meena, read from Maya Angelou. In keeping with our respective Indian and Jewish heritage, I put a flower garland around Doug's neck, and he stomped on a glass. And then it was done.

Cole, Ella, and I agreed that we didn't like the term "step-mom." Instead they call me their "Momala."

One of my favorite family routines is Sunday family dinner. This is a routine I started once Doug and I got engaged. When he and I first started dating, he was a single dad sharing custody with Kerstin. Family dinner had been Chinese takeout and plastic forks, which the kids spirited off to their bedrooms. I changed that. Now everyone knows that Sunday family dinner is a must, that we come together, all of us around the table, relatives and friends always welcome, and I cook a meal for us to share. It's really important to me.

Everyone quickly got into the routine and found their role to play. Cole sets the table, picks the music, and pitches in as an assistant chef in the kitchen. Ella makes restaurant-quality guacamole and exquisite desserts. Doug bought himself a pair of onion goggles, which he dons with great fanfare when it's time to chop.

I make the main dish. It doesn't always go as planned: sometimes the pizza dough doesn't rise or the sauce won't thicken or we're missing a key ingredient and I have to improvise. That's all okay. Sunday family dinner is about something more than the meal.

When dinner is finished, the kids do the dishes. I once told them the story of Uncle Freddy. Because he lived in a small basement apartment in Harlem with a tiny kitchen, Uncle Freddy would clean every single dish or utensil he used as soon as he was done using it. And in time, the kids turned "Uncle Freddy" into a verb. When it's time to clean, they promise to "Uncle Freddy" the place. And they do a pretty good job!

I know that not everyone likes to cook, but it's centering for me. And as long as I'm making Sunday family dinner, I know I'm in control of my life—doing something that matters for the people I love, so we can share that quality time together.

Five

I SAY WE FIGHT

I'll always remember how I felt in November 1992, as a twenty-eight-year-old prosecutor, driving across the bridge from my home in Oakland into San Francisco to celebrate the victory of newly elected U.S. senators Barbara Boxer and Dianne Feinstein. They were the first female senators from California, and the first two women to represent any state at the same time. Their election was a highlight of the so-called Year of the Woman, and an inspiration to girls and women everywhere, including me.

I recalled that celebration twenty-two years later when, in early January 2015, Senator Boxer announced that she wouldn't be running for reelection.

November 2016 was almost two years away, but I had a decision to make. Should I run to replace Senator Boxer?

Becoming a U.S. senator would be a natural extension of the work I was already doing—fighting for families facing soaring housing costs and diminishing opportunity; for people imprisoned in a broken criminal justice system; for students burdened by skyrocketing college tuition; for victims of dishonest companies that tricked them; for immigrant communities, for women, for older people. I knew it was important to bring these priorities to the national level, and I decided I could do it. I announced my candidacy on January 13, 2015. Eventually, so did thirty-three others. Doug, for whom it was his first major campaign, had to get used to a new kind of spotlight.

I tackled the race as I had every other, meeting as many people as I could, listening carefully to their concerns, mapping a plan of action to address them. As the campaign rolled on, my team and I crisscrossed the state in what we called the Kamoji bus, because of the giant emoji caricature of me painted on the back door.

The two-year campaign passed both fast and slow. But even as I focused on my state, my campaign, and the work before me, something ugly and alarming was infecting the presidential election, which was also coming up in November 2016. The Republican presidential primary, to choose the Republican who would face the Democratic presidential nominee in November, was turning into a race to the bottom—a race to anger, a race to blame, a race to fan the flames of discrimination and fear of people who seem different. And the man who prevailed crossed every boundary of decency and integrity—bragging about attacking women; mocking people with disabilities; spewing racism; demonizing immigrants; taunting war heroes and their families; and fueling hostility, even hatred, toward reporters.

As a result, even though I won my race, Election Night 2016 was not a night for cheering. We didn't even have the luxury to catch our breath. We had to turn directly to the new fight before us—a fight against the policies of the new president. Drawing on the words of Coretta Scott King, the widow of Dr. Martin Luther King Jr., I reminded the audience in my victory speech that freedom must be fought for and won by every generation.

"It is the very nature of this fight for civil rights and justice and equality that whatever gains we make, they will not be permanent. So we must be vigilant," I said. "Understanding that, do not despair. Do not be overwhelmed. Do not throw up our hands when it is time to roll up our sleeves and fight for who we are."

I didn't know, when I spoke to my supporters that night,

exactly what was to come. But I did know this: we would need to stand strong and stand together.

On Thursday, November 10, less than forty-eight hours after my election, I visited the headquarters of the Coalition for Humane Immigrant Rights of Los Angeles (CHIRLA).

CHIRLA is one of the oldest immigrant rights advocacy organizations in Los Angeles. It was founded in 1986 to teach immigrants about how they could apply for legal status to become U.S. citizens and about their rights to work. It trained community organizers, challenged anti-immigrant laws, and stood up to discrimination based on national origin (the country an immigrant's family came from). It was the first place I wanted to speak officially as senator-elect.

The room was full. It was full of strong, brave women—young women to mothers to grandmothers to great-grandmothers—working women who did everything from house-cleaning to taking care of the elderly, some of whom spoke fluent English and some of whom spoke only Spanish, all of them ready to fight.

In their courage, their dignity, and their determination, they reminded me of my mother. Standing among them, I thought about the immigrant experience in America.

On the one hand, it's an experience of hopefulness and

purpose, a deep belief in the power of the American Dream—an experience of possibility. At the same time, it's an experience too often scarred by stereotyping and discrimination, both in the open and under the surface.

My mother was the strongest person I have ever known, but I always felt protective of her, too. In part, I suppose, that instinct to protect comes from being the older child. But I also knew my mother was a target. I saw it, and it made me mad. I have too many memories of my brilliant mother being treated as though she were dumb because of her accent. Memories of her being followed around a department store with suspicion, because surely a brown-skinned woman like her couldn't afford the dress or blouse that she had chosen.

I also remember how seriously she took any meeting with government officials. Whenever we would come back from traveling abroad, my mother made sure Maya and I were on our best behavior as we went through the customs line at the airport where you have to show your passport. "Stand up straight. Don't laugh. Don't fidget. Have all your stuff. Be prepared." She knew that every word she spoke would be judged, and she wanted us to be ready. The first time Doug and I went through customs together, these memories kicked in. I was preparing myself in the usual way, making sure we had everything just right and in order. Meanwhile, Doug was as relaxed as ever. It frustrated me that he was so casual. He was genuinely perplexed, innocently wondering, "What's the problem?" We had been raised in different realities. It was eye-opening for us both.

For as long as ours has been a nation of immigrants, we have been a nation that fears immigrants. In the mid-1850s, the first significant third-party movement in the United States, the so-called Know-Nothing Party, rose to popularity on an anti-immigrant platform. In 1882, an act of Congress banned Chinese immigrants to the country. In 1917, Congress established a host of new restrictions on immigrants, including a requirement that immigrants would have to know how to read. In 1924, the number of newcomers allowed into the country from Southern and Eastern Europe was cut dramatically. In 1939, nearly 1,000 German Jews fleeing the Nazis in a ship called the *St. Louis* were turned away from the United States. A plan to allow 20,000 Jewish refugee children into the country was outright rejected. And shortly after, the U.S. government interned some 117,000 people of Japanese ancestry—the government tore these Americans from their homes and communities and forced them to live in internment camps during the war, as if they were enemies or spies or prisoners of war, simply because their families had roots in Japan.

More recently, we have been grappling with globalization. Companies that once had mostly Americans working in businesses located in the U.S. started moving overseas, taking jobs with them. This has made people feel afraid and insecure about their ability to hold on to their job and their way of life. When the Great Recession hit around 2007, it caused massive job losses in America. A number of Republican politicians pointed to immigration as the problem, even as they opposed a law that would have created new jobs. Immigrants have helped shape this country, but they've also become convenient targets for blame, scapegoated for problems they didn't create.

Our country was built by many hands, by people from every part of the world. Immigrants and their children were the creative minds behind many of our best-known brands— from Levi Strauss to Estée Lauder. Sergey Brin, the co-founder of Google, was a Russian immigrant. Jerry Yang, co-founder of Yahoo!, came here from Taiwan. Mike Krieger, the co-founder of Instagram, is an immigrant from Brazil. Arianna Huffington, co-founder of *The Huffington Post*, was born in Greece. In fact, in 2016, researchers found that more than half of Silicon Valley's billion-dollar start-ups were founded by one or more immigrants.

I stood by the podium at CHIRLA, with an American flag

and stars-and-stripes balloons in the backdrop, as a mother—a house cleaner from the San Fernando Valley—spoke in Spanish about her fears of deportation, of being sent back to the country she had escaped. I could barely translate her words, but I understood their meaning and I could feel her anguish. It was visible in her eyes, in her posture. She wanted to be able to tell her children that everything would be okay, but she knew she couldn't.

I thought of the nearly six million American children who live in a home with at least one "undocumented" family member—someone who came to America from another country but didn't file all the proper papers to be here legally—and the trauma and stress that the election had brought them. I had heard many stories of safety plans that were being put in place—mothers telling their children, "If Mommy doesn't come home right after work, call your aunt or uncle to come and get you." How's a kid supposed to focus on classwork or sports or homework when deep in her gut she worries that her mom or dad will disappear?

Advocates working with families told us how children were afraid to go to school, not knowing if their parents would still be there when they got home. Parents canceled their children's pediatrician appointments out of fear that the Immigration and Customs Enforcement Agency (ICE) would be waiting for them. And what would happen to American-born children whose immigrant parents were deported? Should the children stay with a relative in the United States? Should they go with their parents to a country that they had never known? Either option was heartbreaking to imagine.

And then there were questions about immigrants who had been brought to the United States as children but were undocumented. They came here through no fault of their own and knew no other home but America. President Obama had created a program called Deferred Action for Childhood Arrivals (DACA) to protect them from deportation and help them get work permits. But the incoming administration wanted to kill the program, and in so doing, throw the futures of thousands of young people into limbo.

"We are going to fight for the ideals of this country," I told the audience at CHIRLA, "and we are not going to let up until we have won."

I left CHIRLA two days after the election feeling both encouraged and worried. I knew we were preparing for battle together. But I knew, too, that we were underdogs in the fight. We were going to have to steel ourselves for all that was to come.

* * *

Things moved very quickly. The following week, Doug and I flew across the country to Washington for the new senators' orientation. A bipartisan group of senators—senators from both the Republican and the Democratic parties—and their spouses hosted us for three jam-packed days of sessions, during which we were informed about Senate rules and procedures, ethics, and how to set up a Senate office. Doug studied the spouses' binder like a scholar.

Senators play a number of important roles, and my team and I had just under two months between Election Day and New Year's to build the office virtually from scratch. As members of the legislative branch, senators make laws, so I needed policy staff who were experts on every issue that could come up—like relations with foreign countries, the details of health care law, how to fund schools, and a million other topics. Senators also have to help their constituents—in my case 39 million Californians—navigate the federal government. That includes helping veterans who depend on disability payments due to an injury caused in battle, or immigrants who hit a glitch filing their papers to become citizens, or ill senior citizens who need nursing care. My constituent affairs staff would need to start right away to help Californians whose problems couldn't wait. And there are other positions as well—communications staff who respond to reporters' questions, correspondence staff who reply to letters and emails, interns and volunteers that help the whole office run, and more. Hiring a diverse staff was important to me—veterans, women, people of color. I wanted my staff in Washington and our state offices to reflect the people we represent.

The hardest part of the new job for me was being away from Ella. Before becoming a senator, I had gone to every one of her swim meets, every one of her basketball games. Kerstin and I usually embarrassed Ella as we sat together and loudly cheered her name. I hated that I would have to miss some of those games now. And I hated that we would have so much less quality time in person, especially because she was about to go off to college, as Cole had done several years earlier. I was committed to flying home as many weekends as I could, which was important to me for so many reasons—to see my constituents, feel the pulse on the ground, and, crucially, cook Sunday family dinner.

The worst was several months later when I realized I wasn't going to be able to go to Ella's high school graduation because of an important Senate Intelligence Committee hearing that same day. When I called to tell her, she was so understanding, but I felt awful about it. I had conversations with some of my female colleagues afterward. Maggie Hassan, a senator from New Hampshire, bucked me up. "Our kids love us for who we are and the sacrifices we make," she said. "They get it." In the case of Ella and Cole, I'm so lucky to know that's true. When the hearing was over, I dashed to the airport and flew back to California. I missed the graduation ceremony but made it home in time for family dinner that night.

Doug and I rented a temporary apartment in Washington, DC, not far from the Capitol, along with minimal furniture—a pair of stools, a bed, a foldout couch for when the kids came to visit, and, for Doug, a big-screen TV. With things happening so quickly, there wasn't much time on the margins for grocery shopping or cooking, though I did make turkey chili one night and froze enough to last us for weeks.

I was sworn in on January 3, 2017, by Vice President Joe Biden during his final month in office, and moved into a basement office alongside other newly elected senators to start my committee work. Senators sit on committees where they use their specific experience to delve deeply into the topics those committees cover. Most bills start in committees. After they pass a committee, they go to the Senate floor for a vote by all one hundred senators. A bill that has been passed by the Senate and by the House of Representatives then moves on to be signed by the President of the United States to become law. Senate committees also hold hearings and invite outside experts to tell us more about a proposed change to a law. Committees also have the Constitutional duty to approve (or disapprove) of men and women the president appoints to lead cabinet agencies, like the State Department or the Treasury Department or the Department of Homeland Security. And sometimes committees investigate something fishy going on in the president's administration. This is important because the Congress is a coequal branch of government, and we have the Constitutional authority and responsibility to hold the president and all the members of his administration to account. If they're doing something wrong, we the people must figure it out, which we do through our senators and members of Congress. While not every Senate committee had open spots, I was appointed to four based on my expertise and background: Intelligence, Homeland Security, Budget, and Environment and Public Works.

One week later, the Homeland Security Committee held a confirmation hearing for General John Kelly, who had been nominated for secretary of Homeland Security. I chose to focus my questions to him about the DACA program.

"Hundreds of thousands of DACA recipients around the

country are afraid right now for what this incoming administration might do to them and also what it might do to their
unauthorized family members," I said.

Not just anyone could qualify for the program. DACA
recipients had submitted extensive paperwork to the federal
government, including detailed information about themselves
and their loved ones. They had to be in school or have already
earned a high school diploma or certificate, or been honorably
discharged from the armed forces. They had to provide proof
of identity, proof of time and admission in the United States,
proof of school completion or military status, and biometric
information, like fingerprints. Only if they cleared this extensive vetting would they get DACA status.

"These young people," I said to General Kelly, "are now
worried that the information they provided in good faith to
our government may now be used to track them down and lead
to their removal.

"Do you agree that we would not use this information
against them?" I asked. Kelly wouldn't directly answer the
question or any of the other questions I pressed him on.

In the end, I voted against John Kelly's confirmation and
pressed my colleagues to do the same. He wasn't prepared to
keep the nation's promises, and I wasn't prepared to put him in

charge of them. He got confirmed anyway, though, and in the first hundred days of the administration, immigration arrests increased by more than 37 percent. Due to new policy priorities, arrests of undocumented immigrants with no criminal record nearly doubled.

These policies have had far-reaching consequences for children whose parents are locked up. In 2016, a quarter of all kids in the United States under the age of five lived in immigrant families. These children have had to live in the grip of the fear that, at any moment, their parents could be abruptly taken away from them.

Children of immigrants also faced a new kind of torment: bullying. Kids are being taunted by other kids, told they will be deported, told their parents will be deported, told they should go back where they came from. The cruel words and actions of one prominent, powerful bully in the White House have been mimicked and adopted as the rallying cry of bullies everywhere.

But how do you handle a bully? You stand up to him.

In the run-up to Inauguration Day, activists had planned a Women's March in cities all across the country for the day after the official presidential transition as a rebuke to all the nastiness and bullying that we'd collectively endured all through the presidential election and since Election Day. No one could know how it would turn out, but it was huge—beyond all expectations. More than four million people showed up in the streets nationwide, with sister marches in countries around the world.

In Washington, the crowd was so massive that it packed the entire route, end to end—a vibrant sea of pink-hatted people, the symbol of the march, representing the full range of American diversity.

I saw white-haired grandmothers and blue-haired college students; flannel-clad hipsters and down-jacketed soccer moms; toddlers in strollers and teenagers in the trees; men and women in solidarity, side by side. Amazingly, amid the throng, I ran into Aunt Lenore, who engulfed me in a giant bear hug. She told me that her daughter Lilah was in the crowd as well. They had come out to march together, carrying forward the banner of social justice that Lenore and my mother had held high as students at Berkeley half a century before.

I had been asked to speak, and as I climbed up to the stage, I was overwhelmed by the size and spirit of the crowd stretching out before me as far as I could see. There were so many people that cell phone networks had gone down, yet the energy was electric. No one could move, but everyone seemed to understand that the march was a glimpse of a new kind of coalition whose true strength had yet to be tested. "Even if you're not sitting in the White House, even if you are not a member of the United States Congress . . . you have the power. And we the people have the power!" I told the marchers. "And there is nothing more powerful than a group of determined sistahs, marching alongside with their partners and their determined sons and brothers and fathers, standing up for what we know is right!"

Six

WE ARE BETTER THAN THIS

On February 16, 2017, I gave my very first speech on the floor of the United States Senate. It was a humbling experience. In recent years, the Senate hasn't been able to get much done because senators from the two political parties have been unable to seek common ground. Once admired for its culture of thoughtful debate, the Senate has often proved to be anything but. And yet as I stood there, it was the giants of the Senate's past who came to mind, and the extraordinary work that had been done on that very floor. At my Senate desk once sat Eugene McCarthy, who sponsored a 1965 immigration law that established rules aimed at reunifying immigrant families.

I opened my speech exactly as those who know me would have expected. "Above all, I rise today with a sense of gratitude for all those upon whose shoulders we stand. For me, it starts with my mother, Shyamala Harris."

I told her immigration story, the story of her determination, the story that made Maya and me, and made us Americans. "And I know she's looking down on us today. And, knowing my mother, she's probably saying, 'Kamala, what on earth is going on down there? We have got to stand up for our values!'"

I talked about actions by this president that hit our immigrant and religious communities like a cold front, "striking a chilling fear in the hearts of millions of good, hardworking people." The administration was targeting all immigrants. It had even banned people from entering this country who were coming from seven mostly Muslim countries. It was not only chaotic and ill-planned, it was discriminatory and cruel.

I talked about the outsize impact on the state of California, because I believe California is a small-scale version of who we are as Americans. I explained that we have farmers and environmentalists, welders and technologists, Republicans, Democrats, Independents, and more veterans, and more immigrants, than any state in the nation. When it came to DACA, I reiterated what I had said in John Kelly's confirmation hearing: that we had promised recipients that we would not use their personal information against them, and that we could not go back on our promise to these kids and their families.

These policies were more than immoral and heartless, they were dangerous, too. I spoke as a lifelong prosecutor and former attorney general of the largest state in this country when I said that the administration's Muslim ban and immigration actions posed a real and present threat to our public safety. Instead of making us more safe, the increased raids on immigrants and the president's executive orders instill fear. "For this reason," I said, "studies have shown Latinos are more than 40 percent less likely to call 911 when they have been a victim of a crime. This climate of fear drives people underground and into the shadows, making them less likely to report crimes against themselves or others. Fewer victims reporting crime and fewer witnesses coming forward."

I also talked about the economic consequences, noting that immigrants make up 10 percent of California's workforce and contribute $130 billion to our state's economy. "Immigrants own small businesses, they till the land, they care for children and the elderly, they work in our labs, attend our universities, and serve in our military. So these actions are not only cruel. They cause ripple effects that harm our public safety and our economy."

I closed my remarks with a call to action: that we have a responsibility to draw a line and say no—that as a coequal branch of government, it is our duty as members of Congress to uphold the ideals of this country.

The next month, I invited a young woman from Fresno who had graduated from University of California at Merced, a biomedical researcher, and a DACA recipient to be my guest at a joint session of Congress. Yuriana Aguilar's parents moved their family from Mexico to Fresno when Yuriana was just five years old. None of them had papers. Her parents were agricultural workers who supported the family by selling vegetables. Still, as Yuriana recalls, "somehow they knew in order to succeed, you have to have an education." Yuriana took her parents' message to heart—literally. Today she works at Rush Medical College, in Chicago, studying how the heart's electrical system functions. DACA made it possible for her to pursue her education and earn a PhD.

Yuriana has described how, when she first heard about the creation of DACA, she cried with relief. Then she went back to her research, doing her part to help others live healthier lives. As she says, "Science doesn't have borders—there are no limitations on its advancement." My mother would have loved her.

Yuriana's commitment to giving back to our country is typical among DACA recipients. The vast majority of DACA recipients are employed—more than 75 percent of them. They wear our nation's uniform in the military, they study at our colleges and universities, and they work in U.S. companies large and small. In fact, if DACA recipients were deported, it is estimated that the U.S. economy as a whole could lose as much as $460 billion over a decade. These young people are contributing to our country in meaningful ways.

I kept Yuriana top of mind over the course of the drama that would unfold through the year. She was the first person I thought of when, on September 5, 2017, Attorney General Jeff Sessions cruelly and arbitrarily announced that the administration was ending the DACA program, throwing the fates of hundreds of thousands of people into limbo.

Without DACA, eligible young people who were brought to the United States as children are faced with a terrible choice: they can live here without papers and in fear of deportation or leave the only country they've ever known. They have no path to citizenship. They can't leave the country and get in line to immigrate here. There is no line. And for this administration, that's the point.

Congress can fix this. There is bipartisan legislation in the House and the Senate that I've co-sponsored—the DREAM Act—which gives these young people a permanent path to citizenship, a bridge over their otherwise terrible choices. Every day that the DREAM Act goes unpassed is another day that

Dreamers have to live in fear—despite having done everything we asked them to.

I've met many Dreamers over the years, and on a nearly daily basis throughout my first year in the U.S. Senate. They bravely came to Washington to meet with members of Congress and tell their stories. There was one day when I was supposed to meet with five Dreamers from California who were in town as part of a group from all over the country. The others wanted to join, too, so I invited them into my conference room. It was packed, standing room only, with people lined up against the walls.

I was struck by one of the California kids, Sergio, who was a student at the University of California at Irvine. He talked about his mother working in Mexico, unable to make ends meet, and the decision she had made to come to the United States to give him a chance at a better life. He talked about how hard he had worked through school and how he had focused a lot of his energy on doing outreach to help people get health care. Like so many Dreamers, he was taking on a life of service. That's the thing about the Dreamers: they really do believe in the promise of this country. It is their country, too.

There was so much passion in Sergio's eyes. But I knew

he was also frightened. The administration's decision to end DACA had been so dispiriting and demoralizing, so opposite to the better history of our country, and to the promise of opportunity on which he had relied. And as he and most of them searched my eyes, looking for confidence that they would be okay, I fought the pain of knowing how wrong and unfair the situation was, and that I could not, on my own, control the outcome. It pains me still today.

February 2018 was a pivotal month in the immigration fight. The administration continued its cruel and outrageous conduct, going so far as to remove a reference to the United States as "a nation of immigrants" from the mission statement of the agency responsible for citizenship and immigration services. Meanwhile, the administration and many congressional Republicans effectively held the Dreamers hostage, saying they would only agree to vote on the DREAM Act in exchange for the legislation that included $25 billion in taxpayer money to build a wall on the border with Mexico.

There were a number of reasons why I opposed this. Purely from a dollars-and-cents perspective, it was a total waste of taxpayer money. I am a strong believer in border security— but experts agree that a wall will not secure our border.

But there was a bigger reason to oppose the border wall.

A useless wall on the southern border would be nothing more than a symbol, a monument standing in opposition to not just everything I value, but to the fundamental values upon which this country was built. The Statue of Liberty is the monument that defines to the world who we are. Emma Lazarus's poem there includes the words, "Give me your tired, your poor, your huddled masses yearning to breathe free." They speak to our true character: a generous country that respects and embraces those who have made the difficult journey to our shores, often fleeing harm; that sees our optimistic, can-do spirit in those who aspire to make the American Dream their own. How could I vote to build what would be little more than a monument, designed to send the cold, hard message "KEEP OUT"?

And so, the fight on behalf of Dreamers continues. And here's what I believe: These young people were brought into our country, in many cases before they could walk or talk, through no choice of their own. This is the only country they've ever known. This is their home, and they're making a difference here. So I won't let up until they are recognized as the Americans they are.

★ ★ ★

There's a region in Central America known as the Northern Triangle, which includes three countries: El Salvador, Guatemala, and Honduras. Together these countries have the menacing distinction of being among the most violent in the world. Between 1979 and 1992, El Salvador was undone by civil war that left as many as 75,000 dead. Between 1960 and 1996, Guatemala's civil war resulted in the deaths of 200,000 civilians. Honduras didn't have a civil war of its own, but the violence in neighboring countries bled across its borders and made it, too, one of the world's most dangerous places to live. Even after the wars ended, the violence didn't. A broken economy with deep poverty and few jobs, awash in weapons and generational destruction, led to the formation of organized criminal organizations that used murder and sexual violence including rape, the crime of forcing people to have sex against their will, to control territory and take over large swaths of the region. In the years since, more people have been killed and kidnapped in the Northern Triangle than in some of the world's most brutal wars. Between 2011 and 2014, nearly fifty thousand people were murdered in the Northern Triangle, and just 5 percent of the deaths resulted in convictions for the killers in a court of law. For residents of these countries, life is often defined by terror. Gang violence, drug trafficking, and corruption are rampant. Gangs like MS-13 and Mara 18 recruit young men to join their ranks through threats and intimidation, and they force teenage girls to endure sexual violence as so-called gang girlfriends. There are stories of children being robbed, raped, murdered. If there was a ground zero for brutality and bleakness, the Northern Triangle would be it.

The only option is escape. And so hundreds of thousands of people have fled the region into neighboring countries and up through Mexico to the United States. They are refugees seeking asylum, a safe place to land after fleeing the violence of home. In the past, we have welcomed asylum seekers in accordance with international law, granting them special protected status because of the terrible hardships they face. Sometimes they come as families. But all too often, the journey is expensive, leaving parents with an excruciating choice: Do they keep their children close but in the midst of extreme danger, or do they send them to the United States, knowing that if they survive the perilous journey they will have a chance to be safe and free?

In the summer of 2014, tens of thousands of children and adolescents fled the violence of the Northern Triangle through human smuggling networks that brought them to the United States.

I was attorney general of California at the time, sitting at home watching the evening news, when I saw an image that struck a chord. In Murrieta, California—a town roughly halfway between Los Angeles and San Diego—several buses carrying roughly 140 undocumented children and parents were on their way to a processing center. A crowd had gathered, blocking the street, waving flags and signs and yelling, "Nobody wants you!" "You're not welcome!" "Turn around and go back home!" There were children inside the buses, looking out of their windows at faces filled with hate. Their only wrong was that they had fled horrific violence.

And it wasn't just the protesters in the streets. At the same time, a big push was coming out of Washington, DC, to speed up the process of deciding who gets to stay and who gets turned back to their violent homeland. These decisions depend on how kids describe their life before they came to America. That means that children have to share facts and tell their story in a clear way.

I knew, having prosecuted child sexual assault, that in these types of cases, it takes a long time to earn a child's trust, and for a child to be able to tell his or her story in a court of law. What was worse, I learned that these asylum-seeking kids had no right to a lawyer to guide them through the process. And that mattered a great deal. If you don't have a lawyer, there's about a 90 percent chance that you will lose your asylum case. If you have legal advice, there's about a 50 percent chance you will win. Given that deportation would take these children back into the heart of danger, whether or not they had a lawyer was a matter of life and death.

I had to do something about this, and I knew there wasn't any time to waste. So I personally pulled together some of the best lawyers in the state and asked them to come to my office to help me make sure these children, some as young as eight years old, had lawyers, and therefore had access to due process, the right to be treated fairly throughout the court proceeding. Representatives from dozens of law firms met in my conference room in downtown Los Angeles, and I got them to donate their services to help these kids. Then I sponsored legislation to provide $3 million to other organizations that were providing these children with legal representation.

This was my first experience with the crisis in the Northern Triangle and the consequences it had wrought on children and families. But it wouldn't be the last.

Starting right away in January 2017, the new president and his team grasped at any and every measure to bar some of the most needy and helpless people in the world from entering our country. And while we had come to expect disturbing actions out of this White House, even I was shocked by what came next. In March 2017, John Kelly said he was actively considering the possibility of forcing children to be separated from their parents at the border. "I would do almost anything to deter the people from Central America from getting on this very, very dangerous network that brings them up through Mexico into the United States," he said, confirming that it was under consideration.

I questioned him about this outrageous policy at a committee hearing.

"So are you unwilling, sir, to issue a written directive that it is the policy of this department to not separate children from their mothers unless the life of the child is in danger?" I asked.

"I don't need to do that," he replied.

We learned through a *New York Times* report that in the six months between October 2017 and April 2018, seven hundred children had been separated from their parents, including one hundred who were under the age of four.

There are few things more cruel, more inhumane, more evil than ripping a child from her parent's arms. We should all know this to be true on a gut level. But if we needed more proof, we could look at a statement released by Dr. Colleen

Kraft, president of the American Academy of Pediatrics, on behalf of the organization, about the extraordinary stress and trauma of family separation, which "can cause irreparable harm, disrupting a child's brain architecture and affecting his or her short- and long-term health." These findings are shared by the American Medical Association, which has called for an end to the policy, noting that the children the U.S. government is forcibly separating from their parents may be scarred for life.

The administration claimed that it wouldn't separate families seeking asylum if they arrived at an official port of entry—like a border checkpoint—as opposed to other parts of the border. But that wasn't true. There were reports of a six-year-old girl from the Democratic Republic of Congo who was taken from her mother when they arrived at the San Diego port of entry seeking asylum, even though the mother was able to show they were in grave danger. A blind six-year-old was taken from her mother. So was an eighteen-month-old. This wasn't just a tragedy; it was a violation of international law. It was a human rights abuse. And the toll it took was not just on the children. After a man from Honduras was separated from his wife, after his three-year-old son was ripped from his arms, after he was placed in an isolation cell, the trauma led him to take his own life.

Let's call this what it is. The White House and Department of Homeland Security were using children—babies—as hostages in a profoundly misguided and inhumane policy to discourage immigration.

I often describe the balance of our democracy as resting on four legs: three independent, coequal branches of government—the legislative branch (Congress), the executive branch (the presidency), and the judicial branch (the courts)—and a free, independent press. As this horror unfolded, the press worked tirelessly to safeguard our true values. Crews of reporters went down to our southern border, filming and reporting in real time, showing Americans what was really going on, bringing the crisis into our living rooms. The vivid daily coverage informed and inspired a public outcry that eventually forced the administration to backtrack, at least temporarily.

On June 20, 2018, the president signed an executive order that ended its family separation practice. But that did not put an end to the story. Rather than separating families, the new administration policy was to hold those families indefinitely behind bars. As of this writing, jailing innocent children continues to be the policy of the United States. Children remain separated from their parents. And in the aftermath of the executive order, we were still greeted with headlines like this one, from *The Texas Tribune*: "Immigrant Toddlers Ordered to Appear in Court Alone."

On a hot, dry day at the end of June, I visited the Otay Mesa Detention Center, not far from the border between California and Mexico. It was important to ask questions of administration officials in congressional hearings, but equally important to visit with the people who were suffering the consequences of its cruel policies. I've seen many prisons. Otay Mesa was identical in appearance. To get in the facility, which is surrounded by chain-link fences and barbed wire, you have to pass through multiple checkpoints. One gate opens, you stand in the middle area, and then it shuts behind you before another opens ahead. For anyone detained there, it sends a strong signal that you are locked away from the world.

Once inside the building, I met with mothers who'd been separated from their children. They were wearing blue jumpsuits with the word DETAINEE in block letters on their backs. I asked the facility staff to give us some privacy. They stood about twenty yards away while I asked the mothers about their experiences and came to understand the deep trauma they had endured.

Olga told me that she hadn't seen her four children—ages seventeen, sixteen, twelve, and eight—in nearly two months and that she wasn't even sure where they were. She had fled domestic violence, abuse from her partner, in Honduras, taking a flight to Mexico. She stopped at the Tapachula shelter, in Mexico, where she learned that there was a caravan helping asylum seekers get to the United States. It wasn't going to cost her any money, and it was going to drop her off in Tijuana just south of the border. The caravan was a blessing, she told me. They provided her and her family with food on the journey and offered to help her with the process of seeking asylum. She said she traveled by airline, train, and bus and at some points walked, though she was often able to hitchhike. People along the way had wanted to help.

When she arrived in Tijuana, she and her family were taken to churches and shelters, and eventually presented themselves to the U.S. Border Patrol. They were led to a holding cell and told to wait to be processed. That was when her children were taken from her, with no warning or explanation. She pleaded with the Border Patrol agents to tell her where her children had been taken. She presented their birth certificates. She needed answers. Desperately. But no answers were given. All she knew was that her three girls were being held together while her son was all by himself. Eventually a social worker was able to connect her by phone to her kids, who weren't sure exactly where they were. She had come to believe that they were all in New York City, and though they said they were okay, it was hard to imagine that could be true.

The Department of Homeland Security had said that families seeking asylum at ports of entry would not be separated from one another. But when another woman at Otay Mesa, Morena, left El Salvador and presented herself with her two boys—ages twelve and five—at the San Ysidro Land Port of Entry processing center, her children were ripped away from her. She pleaded with the agents not to take her kids, but to no avail. She had to wait fifteen days to call her sons, because detainees were charged eighty-five cents per minute for calls and she didn't have any money. She had to earn some by working at the facility. Morena had worked for seven days straight and was paid only four dollars. Olga had worked for twelve days and was also paid just four dollars. They said that when they tried to report abuse, they were yelled at.

Six weeks had passed and Morena was still unable to get in touch with her children. She called the facility where she was told they'd been taken, but the phone just kept ringing, with no answer. She told me that the only time they were allowed to make phone calls was when their kids were in class and unavailable. Morena said she was finding it hard to eat because she was so distraught over not seeing or speaking to her children in such a long time.

When I spoke with the guards at the detention center, I had a lot of questions, and the answers didn't add up. They told me, for example, that videoconferencing with kids was a service they offered that was available anytime and for free. They assured me that phone calls were free, too. But when I asked the mothers if they knew this, they immediately said no. They didn't even know that videoconferencing was available. And when I returned to Washington and took part in a Judiciary Committee hearing with Matthew Albence, executive associate director of enforcement and removal operations at ICE, the Immigration and Customs Enforcement Agency, our exchange on this topic was revealing.

I told Albence how, during my visit to Otay Mesa, I'd learned from the parents being detained that when they were performing labor, such as cleaning toilets or doing laundry, they were paid one dollar a day. "Are you familiar with that policy? Or practice?" I asked.

"Many of the individuals that are in ICE custody are eligible to apply and work in a voluntary work program," Albence replied. "It's not mandatory; it's voluntary if they choose to do so. Many do choose to do so, just to pass the time, while they're awaiting their hearing or their removal—"

"Do you think that people voluntarily choose to clean toilets to pass their time? Is that what you're saying?"

"I can say that we have a large number of individuals within our custody that volunteer to work in the work program."

"To clean toilets? Sir, is that what you're saying?"

"I don't know every task that these individuals are assigned, but again, it's voluntary."

Voluntary? I don't think so.

The most shocking answer I got during my time at Otay Mesa was when I asked the detention facility staff the question many people had asked me: "Who is responsible for leading the process to reunite these families?"

They looked around at one another blankly for a few seconds, until one (who was apparently more senior than the others) answered, "That would be me." He then admitted that he had no idea what the plan was or the status of any reunification efforts.

We would later learn that federal records linking parents and children had disappeared. In some cases, for unknown reasons, records had actually been destroyed. When a federal court ruled that families had to be reunited within thirty days, government officials had to resort to DNA tests to try to figure out which children belonged with which family.

Before I left the detention facility, I reassured the mothers that they weren't alone—that there were so many people standing with them and fighting for them, and that I would do everything in my power to help them. As I walked down the long driveway toward the exit, I saw that solidarity personified. Hundreds of people had gathered outside the fence, holding vigil in support of the families. People of all ages and backgrounds—children, students, parents, and grandparents— had traveled to Otay Mesa because they shared the anguish and the heartbreak of the mothers inside.

I joined the throng of supporters, many of whom were carrying signs. ESTAMOS CON USTEDES. . . . FAMILIES BELONG TOGETHER. . . . WE WON'T BACK DOWN. Beneath the blazing summer sun, I told the press what I had seen.

"These mothers have given their testimony, if you will, have shared their stories, and they are personal stories of a human rights abuse being committed by the United States government. And we are so much better than this, and we have got to fight against this. This is contrary to all of the principles that we hold dear and that give us a sense of who we are when we are proud to be Americans. But we have no reason to be proud of this."

These mothers had made the dangerous journey to America with their children because they knew that the danger of staying in their home country was even worse. They have the legal right to seek asylum, but when they arrive, we call them criminals. We treat them like criminals. That is not the sign of a civil society, nor is it a sign of compassion. The United States government has brought great shame to the American people.

The values at stake here are so much bigger than an immigration debate.

Nothing makes a child feel more secure than being tucked in by a parent at the end of a day, getting a kiss and a hug, a good-night story, falling asleep to the sound of their voice. Nothing is more important to a parent than talking with their child at night before the child goes to sleep, answering their questions, comforting and reassuring them in the face of any fears, making sure they know that everything will be okay. Parents and children everywhere relate to these rituals. They are part of the human experience.

As family reunification began, we heard horrific stories that showed us just how shameful this administration's actions have been. The *Los Angeles Times* reported on a three-year-old boy who was separated from his father at the border. "At night, Andriy sometimes wakes up screaming in the bunk bed he shares with his mother and baby brother." We saw video of six-year-old Jefferson reunited with his father after nearly two months of separation. The child's body was covered in a rash; his face was bruised; his eyes were vacant. His father cried, enveloping the boy in a hug. Jefferson was stiff and expressionless. We also learned, through *PBS NewsHour*, of a fourteen-month-old who was returned to his parents, after eighty-five days, covered in lice, apparently having not been bathed. It is hard to imagine anything crueler than such blatant state-sponsored child abuse.

A society is judged by the way it treats its children—and history will judge us harshly for this. Most Americans know that already. Most Americans are appalled and ashamed. We are better than this. And we must make right the wrongs that this administration has committed in our name.

Seven

EVERY BODY

"How are you adjusting?" I asked.

"So far so good," Maya replied. "But we haven't had a winter yet."

It was 2008, and Maya was visiting from New York, where she had recently taken a big job at the Ford Foundation. We had lived in different cities before, but for many years our homes were never more than a short car ride away from each other. Now she was almost three thousand miles away. I was adjusting, too.

We were in a restaurant, waiting for our mother, who had asked us to meet her for lunch. All three of us were excited to be back in the same city, even for a brief time. We'd come a long way from the Berkeley flatlands, but we were still Shyamala and the girls.

"The foundation is doing amazing things," she said. "And I'm going to be—"

Maya stopped talking midsentence. She was looking over my shoulder. I turned around. Our mother had just walked in. Mommy—the least vain person I knew—looked like she was ready for a photo shoot. She was dressed in bright silk, clearly wearing makeup (which she never did), her hair professionally blown out. My sister and I exchanged a glance.

"What's going on?" I mouthed to Maya as our mother approached our table. She raised an eyebrow and shrugged. She was just as confused as I was.

We hugged and greeted one another, and our mother sat down. A waiter brought us a basket of bread. We reviewed our menus and ordered our food, making lighthearted conversation.

And then my mother took a deep breath and reached out to us both across the table.

"I've been diagnosed with colon cancer," she said. Cancer. My mother. Please, no.

Even just reflecting back on it now, it fills me with anxiety and dread. It was one of the worst days of my life.

As my mother understood so well from a lifetime of looking at cancer cells under the microscope, no matter who we are or where we are from, our bodies are essentially the same. They work the same way—and they break down the same way, too. No one gets a pass. At some point, nearly all of us will face a profound interaction with the health care system.

So much comes with this realization: pain, worry, depression, fear.

And it is all made worse by the fact that America's health care system is broken. The United States spends more on health care than any other advanced country, but we aren't healthier in exchange. Incredibly, in many parts of the country, life expectancy, how long we can expect to live, is actually shrinking. Meanwhile, working families are overwhelmed by medical bills, a leading cause of financial ruin for many Americans.

I have tremendous respect for the women and men in the medical profession. For so many of them, the call to medicine stems from a deep desire to help others—from helping a baby come into the world to extending the time that person has on earth. But in our nation's approach to health care, we've created a bizarre split: we are home to the most sophisticated medical institutions in the world but the way we pay for health care deprives millions of Americans of equal access to this basic human right. How can that be?

Most of the time, when people go to see a doctor or have a medical procedure, like surgery or an X-ray, they don't pay for it on the spot. It's not like going to a shoe store, paying for sneakers, and walking out owning your new kicks. The way most of us pay for health care is through a middleman: insurance. Most Americans get health insurance coverage for themselves and their families from their jobs. You pay a monthly premium, which is a bill to have the insurance policy, and a co-pay—$25, for example—each time you see your doctor. Because millions of people are paying into the insurance pool, if you get really sick, insurance money starts to pay more for more expensive care.

Unlike many other wealthy nations, the United States government does not provide universal health care—health insurance for all of our citizens—except in a couple of instances: all senior citizens are covered by Medicare, and those who are severely disabled or have very low incomes qualify for the Medicaid program, which pays for their health care.

This system was built on the idea that people could get affordable health insurance coverage for themselves and their families through their jobs. But over the last thirty years, fewer and fewer employers have been providing insurance to workers. That has meant that fewer Americans are covered. And when you don't have health insurance coverage, you're less likely to see a doctor or get medical care until it's an emergency. Most uninsured people can't afford to pay out of pocket for regular checkups that could identify health concerns before they become full-blown problems that are harder to heal and also very costly. Even those who have insurance have seen their premiums rise much faster than their wages, which can mean it's harder for them to afford health care than it used to be. A system where access to medical care depends on how much money you make has created enormous inequalities. A 2016 study found a ten-year gap in life expectancy in America between the wealthiest women and the poorest. The richest women live until about eighty-nine, and the poorest women live until about seventy-nine. That means that being poor reduces your life expectancy more than a lifetime of smoking deadly cigarettes.

The Affordable Care Act (ACA), or Obamacare, went a long way toward making health insurance more accessible and affordable, offering tax credits to those who can't cover their premiums and expanding Medicaid to cover millions of people. But after it passed, Republican leaders worked to sabotage it. They were playing politics with people's lives—and they still are.

There have been more than a hundred lawsuits challenging the ACA since its passage. Republican governors blocked seventeen states from expanding Medicaid, allowing it to cover more people, leaving millions in places like Florida, Texas, Missouri, and Maine without affordable coverage. In numerous states, Republican lawmakers have even passed laws restricting the ability of health care officials to help people enroll in insurance plans, despite a law that provides funding specifically for that purpose.

The new administration joined the fight against providing affordable health care for all Americans. The result? Soaring premiums, forcing people all over the country to give up their health insurance altogether.

And this was on top of the efforts of congressional Republicans to fully repeal the ACA—more than fifty times. In July 2017, their push to end Obamacare was stopped by just three votes—but they will surely try again. If they win, tens of millions of people will lose their health insurance. Repeal would make health care outrageously expensive and it would cut out people who need care the most.

Before the ACA, insurance companies decided how much your premium would cost based on how much of a health risk you were. It sounds like a cold and calculating way to think about our fellow human beings because it is. If you have a preexisting condition—like asthma or diabetes—you will probably need to see the doctor more or get more medicine than someone who is perfectly healthy. That means the insurance company will have to pay more for you. For many years, that also meant insurance companies would charge you more, or deny you coverage altogether. A lot of sick people couldn't get health care. Repealing the ACA would allow insurance companies to do that once again.

And you won't believe some of the things that are considered preexisting conditions.

In early 2011, just after I was elected attorney general of California, I went in to see my dentist for a checkup. The dental hygienist, Chrystal, and I knew each other from past visits, and it had been a while since I'd seen her. Chrystal asked me how I'd been. I told her I'd been elected. I asked her how she'd been. She told me she was pregnant. It was great news.

As a dental hygienist, she was working for a few different dentists but wasn't considered a full-time employee of any of them. This was before the ACA was in place, so Chrystal was on private insurance with only basic coverage—the least expensive plan and the only one she could afford, just enough to cover her yearly checkups. When Chrystal found out she was pregnant, she went to her insurance company to apply for prenatal coverage. To have a healthy baby, she would need to see the doctor more than once a year.

But she was denied. The insurance company told her she had a preexisting condition. I was alarmed.

"You okay? What's wrong?" I asked. "What's the preexisting condition?" And she told me it was that she was pregnant. That was why the insurer had turned her down. When she applied to another health care company for insurance, again she was denied. Why? Preexisting condition. What was it? She was pregnant. I couldn't believe what I was hearing.

This young pregnant woman was forced to wait six months before she received a sonogram to make sure hers was a healthy pregnancy. Thankfully, there was a free clinic in San Francisco where she could get her prenatal care. Thank God Chrystal had a strong and beautiful baby named Jaxxen and they're both doing well today.

But think about that for a minute. This is the world we could return to if they abolish the ACA: women denied health care coverage for continuing the human species. Let's remember the words of Mark Twain: "What, sir, would the people of the earth be without women? They would be scarce, sir, almighty scarce."

The Affordable Care Act provided a lot of relief, but health care is still too costly for working families.

If you've ever had an ear infection or a really bad cough, you've probably taken prescription medication. We need them—to get better, to stop the spread of infection to others, and to save lives. Yet, compared with people in other wealthy countries, Americans face extraordinarily high prescription drug prices. In 2016, for example, the same dose of Crestor, a medication that treats high cholesterol, cost 62 percent more in the United States than just across the border in Canada. This is the case with drug after drug. Three in five Americans take prescription drugs, but one in four of them find their medications difficult to afford.

And drug manufacturers continue to raise prices without a care.

Take pharmaceutical manufacturer Mylan. Mylan raised the price of the EpiPen—a lifesaving treatment for people with allergies so serious they could die—by nearly 500 percent over seven years. Between October 2013 and April 2014, the company jacked up the price of Albuterol, a common treatment for asthma, from $11 to $434. Without it, asthma sufferers cannot get enough oxygen into their bodies. You don't need to be a prosecutor to see something wrong with a 4,000 percent price hike.

Prescription medicines are not luxury goods. Quite the opposite. We don't want to need them! No one aspires to be allergic to peanuts, or to suffer from asthma. I'll always remember the terror I felt when my niece, Meena, had a childhood asthma attack so bad that Maya had to call 911. It's heartless and wrong for companies to make a fortune by exploiting the fact that their customers literally cannot live without their products.

Too many of our fellow Americans are getting crushed under the weight of high drug prices—having to choose between taking the medications they need and buying other things they need to live, like food.

For my mother's cancer treatment, we went through a grim kind of routine. During the day, I would take her to the hospital for chemotherapy. We'd see many of the same people every time—men and women of all different ages, hooked up to a machine that was infusing their bodies with the toxic drugs they hoped would save their lives. It took on a strange familiarity, an abnormal sense of normalcy. If I had to, I'd drop her off and pick her up when chemo was done, but I preferred to wait to keep her company, and she preferred it, too. Sometimes the chemo would steal her appetite. Other times she was hungry, and I would get her buttery croissants that she loved from a bakery nearby. More than once, she had to be admitted to the hospital with complications, and I remember a lot of hard days and nights under those fluorescent lights. When my mother was asleep, I would walk down the long corridors, glancing into the rooms as I passed. Sometimes people would look up. Sometimes they wouldn't. And all too often, they were lying there alone. I left that experience convinced that no one should have to face a hospital stay without support—and that many do.

My mother's circumstance could feel overwhelming. Chemotherapy is draining; oftentimes my mother was too wiped out to do anything but sleep. Meanwhile, there were so many medications, possible side effects, and things to keep track of. What if she had a bad reaction to a new medicine, as happened more than once? I had to coordinate her care, make sure her doctors were talking to one another, and ensure that she was getting the proper treatment. I often wondered how my mother would have fared if we hadn't been there to speak up on her behalf.

I came away believing that all patients deserve advocates with medical expertise so that anyone dealing with a serious illness has a trustworthy, capable champion by their side. After all, we have decided that when their freedom is at stake, people have the right to an attorney. We do this because we understand that most people don't speak the language of the courtroom, and even if they do, in high-pressure situations it's difficult to know what to do. The same is true in a hospital. Emotions are running high. People are placed into a new environment where a specialized language is being spoken, with complex, unfamiliar terms and phrases. And they may have to make decisions while they are frightened or in pain or heavily medicated—or all three. They're expected to be strong enough to monitor themselves at a moment when they feel deeply vulnerable. We should have expert advocates to help out so that patients and their families can focus on healing.

We should also speak truth about the racial inequalities in our health care system. According to a 2015 report, black Americans are more likely to die than any other group in eight of the top ten causes of death. In 2013, the Centers for Disease Control and Prevention reported that black Americans are more likely than white Americans to die of heart disease, cancer, and diabetes (among other conditions), and that their lives are expected to be 3.8 years shorter than those of white Americans.

In segregated cities like Baltimore, there are twenty-year gaps in the life expectancy of those living in poor black American neighborhoods and those living in wealthier and whiter areas. "A baby born in Cheswolde, in Baltimore's far northwest corner, can expect to live until age eighty-seven," writes Olga Khazan in *The Atlantic*. "Nine miles away in Clifton-Berea . . . the life expectancy is sixty-seven, roughly the same as that of Rwanda [in Africa], and twelve years shorter than the American average."

These disparities begin in the delivery room. Black babies are twice as likely as white babies to die in infancy, a stunning gap that is wider than in 1850, when slavery was still legal. In fact, today, black infants are less likely to survive their first year than white babies were in the early 1980s.

Black women are also at least three times as likely to die due to complications relating to pregnancy than white women—a shocking gulf that holds as true for highly educated, wealthier women as for those who are neither. A major five-year study in New York City found that college-educated black women are more likely to face severe complications in pregnancy or childbirth than white women who never made it through high school.

There are a number of factors that put black men, women, and children at a disadvantage. Hundreds of years of discrimination against black Americans in every conceivable area of life—where they could live, who would hire them, the quality of the schools in their neighborhoods—have left black Americans more likely to live in poor neighborhoods with limited healthy food options, and fewer community health care resources.

And because black Americans are more likely than their white counterparts to be born and raised in low-income, high-crime neighborhoods, they are more likely to experience a phenomenon known as toxic stress from witnessing violence or experiencing it. As one researcher discovered, such stress "literally gets under our skin and has the potential to change our health."

One study found that children who experience at least six traumatic childhood experiences have shorter lives—by more than twenty years! Stress increases our blood pressure, which is unhealthy—even deadly—for pregnant women and their babies. Stress actually ages us faster. Research has even found that black women were biologically more than seven years older than white women their age.

It's also the case that black Americans experience poorer care when they go to the doctor. White patients are 10 percent more likely to get screened for high cholesterol than black Americans, even though rates of heart disease and stroke, often caused by elevated cholesterol, are higher among black Americans.

Black patients are also less likely to be treated using procedures to repair blocked arteries. White women are more likely to get breast cancer screenings than black women and Latinas. And women of color are more likely to have their symptoms dismissed by their doctor, regardless of their economic status.

When tennis star Serena Williams, one of the greatest athletes of all time, delivered her baby, she had serious complications. The day after she gave birth, Williams started having trouble breathing. She had a history of blood clots in the artery leading to her lungs and, having experienced them before, she suspected she was having another. She told *Vogue* magazine that she walked out of her hospital room so that her mom wouldn't worry and told her nurse that she needed a CT scan and blood-thinning medication right away. But the nurse was skeptical, and the doctor called for a different procedure. Williams persisted.

When they finally sent her for a CT, they discovered that she was right after all. "I was, like, listen to Dr. Williams!" she told *Vogue*. There were further complications that required surgery and left her bedridden for six weeks. If someone like Serena Williams can go through such an ordeal, imagine what happens to other patients who know what symptoms they're experiencing but are ignored.

What accounts for these inequities in the care of our fellow citizens? A growing body of research suggests that part of the problem is unconscious, implicit bias. All of us absorb social stereotypes and assumptions, often without ever realizing it. But left unexamined, they risk leading us to behave in discriminatory ways, which can have serious consequences.

How do we close the divide? It starts by speaking the uncomfortable truth that it exists, and then we can break the problem into parts we can tackle one by one. First and foremost, we need every medical school in the country to require implicit bias training for their students. When people are given the knowledge that implicit bias is real, and that we all have it, it gives them room to think about it in their daily actions and make better decisions.

We also need medical schools to bring more diversity into the field. As of 2013, only about 9 percent of our country's physicians are nonwhite, and only 4 percent are black. This is the first gap we need to close if we intend to close the others. It won't be easy. It'll be a generational challenge. But it's time we get started.

Most critically, however, improving health outcomes across the board demands that we transform the health care system itself. We need Medicare for All, a new system where everyone, not just senior citizens, could get health insurance through Medicare.

Imagine if U.S. health care coverage was based not on how much you can pay but instead on your health needs. Getting sick would no longer mean having to pay more money than your family can afford. Employers would no longer have to spend so much to provide health insurance to their employees. And the system itself would run far more efficiently.

There are other critical ways to improve our health care system, and one of the most important is to stay on the cutting edge of medical research. That means we need to dramatically increase funding to the National Institutes of Health. My mother once worked with other researchers at the NIH. She spoke of her time there so admiringly that when I was a girl, I imagined Bethesda, Maryland, where the agency is located, to be a place filled with castles and spires. I might have been wrong about the architecture, but not about the beauty of scientific collaboration—and certainly not about the fact that the NIH is a national treasure. If we want our children to have cures for humanity's most terrible diseases, we should invest in our national medical researchers.

Our country has the world's finest medical practitioners, most inventive medical scientists, and most sophisticated technology. But these wonders are out of reach for too many Americans. The most pressing task ahead of us to is to put in place policies, like Medicare for All, to open the doors of our extraordinary health care system to everyone regardless of economic status or race. With hard work and political will, we can fix our broken system. Americans are ready for it.

In the days before being sworn in as senator, I read a newspaper profile of Chillicothe, Ohio, a small city in southeastern Ohio's Ross County. It's located in the foothills of the Appalachian Mountains, with sprawling fields of soybeans and corn and a skyline marked by the smokestacks of a paper mill that has operated continually for more than a hundred years. Kenworth has its largest truck-manufacturing plant in Chillicothe and pays decent wages. The local hospital is one of the county's largest employers. But the grand history and pride that once defined this town have been replaced by a sense of despair.

Seventy-seven thousand people call Ross County home. In 2015 alone, doctors in the county prescribed 1.6 million opioid pills. Opioids are potent painkillers that are related to the drug heroin. They are also highly addictive and extremely dangerous. That same year, thirty-eight people died from accidental overdose. The following year, another forty lost their lives. When opioids become scarce—say a doctor won't prescribe any more or they are too expensive to buy from the pharmacy—people with the addiction turn to heroin, a drug that most take using a needle to shoot the drug directly into their veins. "Now you can get heroin quicker in these communities than you can get pizza," Teri Minney, head of Ross County's Heroin Partnership Project, told *The Washington Post*. "They're delivering." According to the *Post*, addicts in Ross County often shoot up in public places, hoping that if they overdose, paramedics or police officers will revive them. "One day in September, police and paramedics responded to thirteen separate overdose calls, including one fatality: a man who died in an apartment right on Main Street. Meanwhile, a woman overdosed in her car as it idled at a Valero gas station with her two-year-old daughter in the back seat."

As has happened in other areas with heavy opioid use, the violent crime rate has gone up, as have incidents of theft. So have the numbers of opioid-addicted babies born, and of children who needed to be taken from their own homes and put into foster care. According to local officials, two hundred children were placed into state care in 2016, three-quarters of whom had parents with opioid addictions. What was once one of the happiest places in Ohio is now clouded by a fog of hopelessness.

Similar stories are repeating themselves in every state in America. The human toll has rocked the nation to its core. Entire communities have been destroyed.

The opioid epidemic has killed more than 350,000 Americans in the past two decades. But the national health crisis we face today is itself the result of a failure of public health intervention, from the moment the opioid OxyContin was approved to be sold.

In 1996, executives of the company Purdue Pharma, the makers of OxyContin, testified in Congress that the drug wasn't really addictive. They began to market the drug as safe to combat pain, despite the fact that company officials had received information that pills were being crushed and snorted, and that doctors were being charged with the crime of selling prescriptions to addicted patients. Doctors were prescribing more and more OxyContin every year.

By 2012, sixteen years after OxyContin reached the market, health care providers had written 259 million prescriptions for opioids. For perspective, there are about 126 million households in America.

According to the National Institutes of Health, roughly 80 percent of Americans who become addicted to heroin start with a prescription for opioids. The danger worsened in 2013 as fentanyl, an exceptionally deadly man-made opioid with fifty times the strength of heroin, made its way from China into the American heroin supply.

How has the federal government responded? Not in the way one would hope.

In 2017, the administration declared the opioid crisis a public health emergency, but the fund they used to deal with it had only—I kid you not—$57,000 in it. That's about a quarter of what it would cost to buy a home—one home—in America, and it doesn't even pay for two years at a private college for one student. It represents less than one dollar for each person who died of a drug overdose that year. It's absurd. And if Republicans had succeeded in repealing the Affordable Care Act, they would have taken addiction treatment coverage away from three million Americans.

This is a crisis that deserves a major federal mobilization. We need to declare a national state of emergency, which would provide more funding, right away, to help combat this disease— giving places like Chillicothe, Ohio, more resources to pay for addiction treatment, hospital services, skills training, and more.

Finally, we need to understand that, at its core, this is a public health issue. It is normal human behavior to want to stop feeling pain, whether physical or emotional, and people will find ways to do so. Sometimes that will mean getting help, and sometimes it will mean getting hooked on heroin. Our job is not to punish our friends and family members and neighbors by throwing them in prison for being addicted to drugs. It is to put them on a healthy path to better manage their pain.

As my mother's condition worsened, she needed more care than we could provide her. We wanted to hire a home health care aide to help her—and me. But my mother didn't want help.

"I'm fine. I don't need anybody," she would say, even though she could barely get out of bed. There was a fight to be had about it, but I didn't want to have it. Cancer—the disease she'd devoted her life to defeating—was now wreaking its havoc on her. Her body was giving out. The medication was making it difficult for her to function—to be herself. I didn't want to be the one who took her dignity away.

So we muddled through. I cooked elaborate meals for her, filling the house with the smells of childhood, which reminded us both of happier times. When I wasn't at the district attorney's office, I was most often with her, telling stories, holding hands, helping her through the misery of chemotherapy. I bought her hats after she lost her hair, and soft clothes to make her as comfortable as I could.

There isn't a smooth, steady decline, I would learn. The process isn't gradual. My mother would reach a plateau and stay there for weeks or months, then, seemingly overnight, fall to the plateau beneath it. During one especially hard spell, I convinced her to spend two weeks at the Jewish Home for the Aged—a place known for some of the kindest and best care—where she could get the round-the-clock attention she needed. We packed her up and drove over to the home. The staff was incredibly kind to our family. They gave my mother a tour of the facility, showed her to her room, introduced her to the doctors and nurses, and explained the routine of her care.

At one point, one of the doctors pulled me aside. "How's my DA?" she asked. The question caught me off guard. She was asking about me. I had been so focused on my mother's well-being I hadn't made room for anything else, but the question cracked through the strength I had mustered. I started to choke up. I was scared. I was sad. Most of all, I wasn't ready.

She asked me if I had heard of "anticipatory grief." I hadn't, but the term made perfect sense. So much of me was in denial. I couldn't bring myself to believe that I was going to have to say goodbye. But underneath it, I was aware. And I had started grieving my mother's loss already. Talking to the doctor helped me understand what was happening to me. Putting a label on things can help you cope with them, I've learned. It doesn't make you stop feeling your emotion, but you can put it somewhere if you can name it. And now I could.

When the tour was over, I unzipped my mother's suitcase so that I could help her move in. But she had other plans. She was sitting cross-legged on the bed, all five feet of her, when she said firmly, "Okay, this was nice. Let's leave."

"Mommy, you're going to stay here for two weeks, remember?"

"No, I'm not. Nn-nnn. I'm not staying for two weeks." She turned to the medical team, who were still in the room. "This has been great. Thank you. We're leaving."

And so we did.

She ended up in the hospital not long after that. That was when I started to see another change. For as long as I could remember, my mother loved to watch the news and read the newspaper. When Maya and I were kids, she'd insist we sit down in front of television news each night before dinner. She loved to digest everything that was happening in the world. But suddenly, she had no interest. Her mighty brain had decided it had had enough. Though she still had room for us.

I remember that I had just gotten into the attorney general's race and she asked me how it was going.

"Mommy, these guys are saying they're gonna kick my butt."

My mother had been lying on her side. She rolled over, looked at me, and just unveiled the biggest smile. She knew who she had raised. She knew her fighting spirit was alive and well inside me.

But then it came time for hospice care, a final round of care at the end of a patient's life that keeps them as pain-free and comfortable as possible. We took her home and, finally, she let a hospice nurse come with us. Maya and I still didn't believe that she could die, to the point that when she said she wanted to go to India, we booked plane tickets and started planning. We worked out how we could get her on a plane, and made arrangements for a nurse to come with us. We were all in a great state of delusion—especially me. I couldn't bear to tell my mother no—not because she couldn't take it, but because I couldn't. Whether it was a question of bringing a nurse home or staying in the nursing home or going to India, I didn't want to accept what saying no to her meant. I didn't want to accept that she was running out of time.

One night, we were all at my mother's house when Aunt Mary and Aunt Lenore, who had flown into town, came for a visit. I decided to cook again. I'll never forget that night—I was making beef stew. I had browned the cubes of beef and they were cooking down in red wine, and all of a sudden my brain figured out what was happening around me. I started to hyperventilate—short breaths in and out. I felt like I might faint. All of a sudden, I had to face reality. I was going to lose my mother and there was nothing I could do.

We had called our uncle in India to let him know that she was too sick to make it. He got on a plane from Delhi to see her. I now realize that she waited for his arrival, waited to say goodbye. She passed away the very next morning.

One of the last questions she asked the hospice nurse, the last concern on her mind, was "Are my daughters going to be okay?" She was focused on being our mother until the very end.

And though I miss her every day, I carry her with me wherever I go. I think of her all the time. Sometimes I look up and talk to her. I love her so much. And there is no title or honor on earth I'll treasure more than to say I am Shyamala Gopalan Harris's daughter. That is the truth I hold dearest of all.

Eight

THE COST OF LIVING

When I think about my mother now, one of the strongest images that comes to mind is that of her hands—always in motion, always productive. Our mother loved to talk with her hands, and she was always using her hands—to cook, to clean, to comfort. She was always busy. Work itself was something to value—hard work especially; and she made sure that we, her daughters, internalized that message and the importance of working with purpose.

When Maya and I were little we loved watching TV. To make sure that we didn't just fritter away our time sitting in front of the tube, my mother taught us how to crochet to keep our hands busy, even if our eyes were glued to the screen. Needless to say, TV time was no longer wasted—we produced piles and piles of pot holders and embroidered wall-hangings.

She also showed us, in so many ways, how much she valued all work, not just her own. When something good would happen at the lab, my mother would come home with flowers for our babysitter.

"I wouldn't have been able to do what I did if you didn't do what you do," she would say. "Thank you for everything."

She saw the dignity in the work that society requires to function. She believed that everyone deserves respect for the work they do, and that hard effort should be rewarded and honored.

I'd hear the same thing at Rainbow Sign, where speakers would talk about Dr. Martin Luther King Jr.'s Poor People's Campaign, about his belief that "all labor has dignity," and his effort to make it so.

As part of that effort, Dr. King had gone to Memphis in 1968 to join black sanitation workers in their fight for basic decency. Day in and day out, these workers rode the trucks that hauled away the city's garbage. The city didn't provide uniforms; instead, workers were forced to dirty their own clothes on the job. They worked long hours without water to drink or a place to wash their hands. "Most of the tubs had holes in them," one sanitation worker recounted. "Garbage leaking all over you." He described how, when the workers got home in the evening, they'd remove their shoes and clothes at the door and maggots would fall out.

For this hard, crucial work, they received little more than

minimum wage, the lowest possible wage that the government will allow employers to pay. They didn't get overtime pay. They had no sick leave. If they were injured at work and needed time to heal—as happened often—they were likely to be fired. And if bad weather made trash collection impossible, they were sent home without pay. Many didn't make enough money to feed their families.

When the city refused to pay the families of two sanitation workers who were crushed to death by their trash compactor, it became too much for the others to bear. With great courage, 1,300 Memphis sanitation workers went on strike, refusing to work while demanding safer conditions, better pay and benefits, and recognition of their union. They were on strike for their families, for their children, and for themselves. It was, above all else, a battle for dignity. The signs they held at marches said simply I AM A MAN.

When Dr. King arrived at Bishop Charles Mason Temple, in Memphis, on March 18, 1968, a crowd of 25,000 people had gathered to hear him speak.

"So often we overlook the work and the significance of those who are not in professional jobs, of those who are not in the so-called big jobs," he said. "But let me say to you tonight, that whenever you are engaged in work that serves humanity and is for the building of humanity, it has dignity and it has worth.

"We are tired," Dr. King said to the audience in Memphis. "We are tired of our children having to attend overcrowded, inferior, quality-less schools. We are tired of having to live in dilapidated substandard housing conditions. . . . We are tired of walking the streets in search of jobs that do not exist . . . of working our hands off and laboring every day and not even making a wage adequate to get the basic necessities of life."

Sixteen days later, Dr. King returned to Memphis to march on behalf of the strikers—speaking again at Bishop Charles Mason Temple, where he declared, "I've been to the mountaintop." The next evening, April 4, 1968, he was killed by an assassin. Two months after that, on June 5, Robert F. Kennedy, brother of the slain President John F. Kennedy, was murdered as well. The nation's clearest voices and strongest leaders in the fight for economic justice had been suddenly and forever silenced.

That was half a century ago. In some ways, we have come so far since then. And in others, we have barely budged. I remind people that when you adjust for inflation—the gradual rise in prices over time—the federal minimum wage is actually lower now than when Dr. King spoke of "starvation wages" in

1968. What does that say about how our country values the sanctity and dignity of work?

Americans are a hardworking bunch. We pride ourselves on our work ethic. And for generations, most of us have been raised to believe that there are few things more honorable than putting in an honest day's work to take care of our family. We grew up trusting that when we worked hard and did well, we would be rewarded for our effort. But the truth is, for most Americans, it hasn't been that way for an awfully long time.

Whenever there is a major push to pressure Congress into doing the right thing, activists and elected leaders beg the American people to call and write their representatives. These days, the phone lines are overwhelmed by Americans engaged in an extraordinary thing: exercising democracy. And it really makes a difference. I believe that the Republican attempt to repeal the Affordable Care Act failed in 2017 because it outraged and energized people to fight back; and because of the pressure they put on key senators, the people prevailed. That means that millions of people still have health coverage because individual Americans—grown-ups and kids—picked up the phone and wrote letters.

For me, reading these letters isn't just about understanding where people stand on major policy issues. It's about understanding what their lives are like, both the joys and the fears. When people write to me, it is often as a last resort. They are struggling, and in real trouble, but nothing else they've tried has worked. And so they reach out to me and share with me the things that keep them up at night.

Dear Senator Harris,

>*My husband and I work full time jobs yet we still struggle every week to make ends meet. I get full [health care] coverage for my two-year-old son [for] which I thank God every day, but can't figure out why my husband and I can't get full coverage either?*
>
>*. . . We can't get help with daycare because we "make too much money" but yet we can't even afford to pay $50 a month for daycare, so we depend on family, [but] they have their own problems, so there have been too many occasions [when] we lose money because we can't get a babysitter for us to go to work.*

. . . I am begging with my life that this needs to change!! Please for the love of God HELP!! This is just not ok! I am confused, angry, frustrated, and I feel so betrayed by our government! I don't EVER ask for help unless I need it and I seriously need it!!

Every letter stands on its own. But together, they tell the same story. It is the story of Americans trapped in a cost-of-living crisis, where their bills for housing and health care and child care and education are way higher than they used to be while wages remain as low as they've been for decades. Basically, you keep making the same amount of money, but what you buy costs more and more each year. When it comes to making a living, Americans are often sectioned into economic classes—the upper class is rich, the working class is poor, and then, right in between, is the middle class, a fuzzy description that is where most Americans place themselves. In an ideal sense, the middle class is made up of people who have steady jobs and earn a decent enough wage to live in a comfortable, though not fancy, home, in a safe neighborhood with good schools and nearby playgrounds for their kids. The driving principle of the middle class is that if you work hard and play by the rules, your kids will grow up better off than you were. But the letters I receive consistently tell the story of the hollowing out of the middle class, and of an economic life defined by intense struggle, and fears about the future.

When I wake up in the middle of the night with a worry on my mind, I remind myself that in countless households around the country, someone else is wide-awake, too. Millions of someone elses. And I imagine that the majority of them are asking themselves questions about their greatest fears: Am I going to be able to provide a good life for my kids? What if I can never make ends meet? How will I get my income to stretch through all my bills this month?

The American people have not given up on the American Dream. I know this to be true. But when you can't sleep at night, how can you dream?

How can you dream when, on average, a year of child care for a baby or toddler is more expensive than a year of in-state public college tuition? How can you dream when the cost of higher education—colleges and universities—has gone up more than three times faster than wages since I was in school in the eighties? How can you dream when you are drowning in student loan debt to pay for the education you need in order to get a good job?

How can you dream if you make minimum wage and work forty hours a week, knowing that, in 99 percent of U.S. counties, you can't afford the going rent on the average one-bedroom apartment?

How can you dream when your pay barely budges no matter how hard you work, while everything else keeps getting so much more expensive and your bills keep piling up? How can you dream when you're a mom whose son is sick but you can't afford your co-pay for a doctor visit?

A middle-class life isn't what it used to be where parents could make enough money to afford the basics for their families. And right now it isn't what it's supposed to be. Being middle-class ought to mean having financial security and stability. But how is that possible when the cost of living is so high that you live on the edge of catastrophe? An injury. An illness. Nobody expects life to be easy, but it's not supposed to be as hard as it is right now.

I often think of Mr. and Mrs. Shelton. She was a nursery school teacher and he was a construction worker, and on those incomes they were able to purchase a two-bedroom home that was everything they dreamed of, and everything they had worked for. But at the time of this writing, that house is listed on a home-selling website at close to a million dollars, which would be impossible to purchase on the salaries of a teacher and a construction worker. These out-of-control housing costs are a problem in cities all across the country, like Denver and Phoenix, where less than 1 percent of the homes on the market were affordable on the average teacher's salary.

In rural areas, housing is more affordable, but that doesn't help since there aren't jobs. According to a recent report, only 3 percent of job growth in the twenty-first century has come from rural areas. So people have an awful choice: endure a long commute every day, or move away from the place where their family has lived for a generation, the place where their friends live, where their kids play little league baseball, where they have always gone to church.

I also think of the workers I've met along the way whose work is worth way more than they're paid. Several years ago, I met a woman named Wendy and got to spend the day with her, watching her work up close. She had changed jobs when her elderly mother got sick, becoming a home health care worker so she could be the one to take care of her day and night. That meant everything from lifting her mother out of her bed to dressing her, feeding her, assisting her in the bathroom, measuring and tracking her blood pressure and body temperature, helping her into her wheelchair and taking her out for a walk, and chatting with her to keep her mom's mind active. It was detailed and demanding work, physically, mentally, and emotionally.

And yet, in 2017, the average home health aide in the United States was earning too little to keep a four-person household out of poverty. What does this say about the value we place on caring for older Americans? What does this say about how we honor our elders?

The cost-of-living crisis is especially hard on women. Women are still paid, on average, eighty cents on the dollar compared with men—a gap that is even more punishing for black American women, who are paid only sixty-three cents for every dollar earned by white men. As the National Women's Law Center points out, that means a black woman who works full time, year-round, comes up more than $21,000 behind her white male counterpart. That affects everyone in her home. It's even worse for Latinas, who make just fifty-four cents on the dollar.

Politicians talk a big game about the value of hard work. But it's time we speak some truth. The truth is that the economy stopped rewarding and valuing most hard work a long time ago. And we've got to acknowledge that if we're going to change it.

Let's start by reflecting on how we got here.

For several decades after the Second World War, workers got pay raises when companies did well. And the government gave people a hand up, offering free education through the GI Bill, which paid for higher education for veterans coming home from the war. The result? Our country grew richer and stronger by leaps and bounds. One of the key measures for this is business productivity. If a candy company can make sweets faster than its competitors or at a lower cost than it used to, it's considered more productive. In the post–World War II economy, productivity rose just about everywhere in the U.S.—a staggering 97 percent improvement. The difference then was that most workers shared in the bounty. During that same period, worker wages grew 90 percent. That's how the United States was able to build the world's largest middle class. Things weren't perfect for everyone. Discrimination against people of color and against women in the workplace and in society were rampant. However, the general orientation of the economy was that growing the middle class was a goal we all shared.

But in the 1970s and '80s, corporate America—the owners of big companies—decided to go its own way. Instead of spending the money the company earned on workers, the corporations decided that their only real obligation was to their shareholders, those who bought company stock and therefore owned a piece of the company. From big business's perspective, it was those owners who deserved the lion's share of the riches, not the people who made the company run. So while productivity kept improving—a whopping 74 percent between 1973 and 2013—workers' pay rose just 9 percent. In the 1980s, President Reagan made that idea core to the Republican Party's view of economics. Cut taxes for corporations. Cut taxes for shareholders. Oppose minimum wage increases for workers. Oppose the very idea of a minimum wage. Crush organized labor—unions—the most powerful force fighting for workers' rights to fair wages and decent working conditions. Roll back government regulation of corporations. Ignore the human cost.

All the while, these companies outsourced and offshored—moved their operations to other countries where they could pay workers even less. Welcome to a new era of selfishness and greed. And it was frighteningly effective. Corporate profits have soared, but American workers haven't gotten a meaningful raise in forty years. And yet there is no shame, it seems, in CEOs making more than three hundred times the wage of their average worker.

The goal of economic growth has to be to grow the pie. But if all that's left for workers are the crumbs, what kind of economy are we really building? This was the context in which we entered the twenty-first century. The jobs were gone. Communities turned into ghost towns.

I read so many letters that underscore the significance of the passage of time. A man, sixty-two, who lost everything in the Great Recession, who has nothing left for retirement and is running out of working years. A couple dealing with a family health crisis, who can't afford to pay their medical bills and still cover the monthly rent. They need help right now; they can't wait. Anyone stuck in a cycle of financial desperation will tell you it's an emergency. That there is no time for delay. Dinner has to go on the table tonight. Gas has to go in the tank in the morning. The bills have to be paid tomorrow. The rent is due at the end of the week. There is truly no time to spare.

According to research done by United Way, 43 percent of households can't afford basic expenses: a roof over their head, food on the table, child care, health care, transportation, and a cell phone.

What are people supposed to think about a government that has left them behind? How are you supposed to feel when you're drowning and no one is coming to your aid, and then you turn on the television and hear that the economy is doing great? Great for whom? It's not great for people who have had to move hours away from their job just to find an affordable place to live. It's not great for people who have stopped working because they can't afford child care. It's not great for the people who are giving up on their dream of going to college because they know they can't afford it.

We are running out of time. That's the hard truth. And not just in terms of dealing with what is so urgent right now, like the gas bill and health emergencies. We are running out of time to deal with major changes to come. As technology continues to take over, more and more people will lose jobs. Take driverless trucks: self-driving trucks could cost 3.5 million truck drivers their jobs. One study suggests that technology could replace 2.5 million jobs in a range of industries each year. We have seen, already, the costs of job loss. But nothing has yet prepared us for what is to come.

We will also have to cope with the realities of climate change. The planet is warming. Scientists agree that it's because humans are spewing too many greenhouse gases—like carbon dioxide and methane—into the atmosphere, which trap the sun's heat. And that warming will mess with the weather, elevate sea levels, and alter life as we know it. In 2017, extreme weather events in America—things like hurricanes, tornadoes, droughts, and floods—killed more than 362 people, forced more than one million to move, and caused more than $300 billion in damage. Experts predict that over time, things will get much worse, but we have the power to act to prevent, reduce, or delay some of the worst outcomes.

Put bluntly, we have work to do. Hard work. We have everything we need—all of the raw ingredients—to build an economy for the twenty-first century that is fair and sturdy, an economy that rewards the work of those who sustain it. But we have to hurry. And we have to be willing to speak truth.

We need to acknowledge that the jobs of the future are going to require people to earn an education after high school that is affordable and prepares them for those jobs.

Let's speak truth about housing costs. We can't have a functioning society if people can't afford to live in it, so we need to enact laws that create more affordable housing and give relief to people who are struggling—right now—to pay their rent.

Let's speak truth about child care. If we don't find a way to make it affordable, we're building barriers too high for parents, and especially women, to participate in the workforce.

And let's speak truth about what we have to build up. We have roads and bridges that need building and upgrading. We have broadband internet infrastructure to build in rural areas that still lack it. We have new wind farms and transmission lines that need installing. We have airports that need modernizing and subways in dire need of repair. Today's grown-ups owe at least this much to our children and grandchildren.

Let's also speak truth about organized labor, which has been systematically taken apart by the Republican Party. In the midst of a Republican effort to hollow out the middle class, it is unions that have successfully forced companies to pay better wages and provide better benefits. We need a rebirth of organized labor in America.

And let's speak one final truth: big corporations and the richest people in the richest country in the world can afford to pay their fair share of taxes so that we can fix the economy. It's necessary, it's moral, and it's wise.

Nine

SMART ON SECURITY

Mysteries and spy thrillers offer a sensational view of intelligence work, but there's a lot more to it than secret agents in trench coats and cameras hidden in handbags. The U.S. intelligence community is made up of seventeen organizations, including the CIA and the FBI. They collect and analyze information that's important for national security—keeping the country safe—and they regularly update a few key players, including the President of the United States and a select group of members of Congress. Often the information is classified, and therefore can't be shared with the wider public, so as not to endanger the agents who collected it and those who shared information with them. This is known as protecting sources and methods (who we got the information from, and how).

When I arrived in the Senate, I joined the Senate Intelligence Committee, fully expecting the work to be done in the shadows and away from the public spotlight. But days after

I was sworn in as a United States senator, those expectations went out the window. On January 6, 2017, the intelligence community released an alarming report: Russia had conducted multiple cyber operations against the United States, with the intent of influencing the outcome of the 2016 presidential election. In other words, Russia hacked the 2016 race for president. Suddenly our work—an investigation into what had gone so terribly wrong—would become some of the most important in the history of the Senate.

Most of what I do on the committee involves classified information that has to remain secret, so there's a real limit to what I can write about here. But there are times when the intelligence community makes reports public, stripped of "sources and methods." I can—and will—reference that work.

Twice a week, for two hours at a time, members of the Intelligence Committee get together behind closed doors to speak with the men and women who lead our seventeen intelligence agencies and receive briefings on the latest information. I can't tell you the details of what we talk about, but I can tell you what it's like. For starters, the room we gather in is known as a SCIF, which stands for Sensitive Compartmented Information Facility. It has been designed to prevent eavesdropping of any kind. Before we enter, we have to put our cell phones in a cupboard outside the door. Inside, we take classified notes by hand, and even those must be kept locked away in the SCIF. When the committee holds public hearings, Democrats sit on one side of the dais and Republicans on the other as we face witnesses and cameras. But inside the SCIF and away from the cameras, it is a very different environment. Often senators take off their jackets. We get down to business. It is not just the absence of cameras and the seating arrangement that change the dynamic; it is the work itself. The rigid divide between Republicans and Democrats that has paralyzed much of Washington somehow fades as we enter the room. There is simply no space for anything other than a focus on America's national security and the protection of Americans' privacy and rights. The public can't be there, nor the media, nor other senators who aren't on the committee. It's just us, to do oversight with global reach. It is invigorating, even inspiring. It is a scene I wish the American people could see, if just for a moment. It is a reminder that even in Washington, some things can be bigger than politics.

My work on the Intelligence Committee and the Homeland Security Committee covers a broad range of issues, from building and maintaining America's ability to fight terrorism at home and abroad to protecting and securing our borders;

to the challenge posed by nuclear weapons; and to the ever delicate balance between gathering intelligence and protecting civil liberties, so that people's freedoms are not trampled by government. But rather than run through the laundry list of issues we deal with in all their complexity, I want to focus on a few of the threats that keep me up at night.

First and foremost, I think of cybersecurity—a new front in a new kind of battle. Our cities aren't being bombed daily by Russian, Chinese, North Korean, and Iranian warplanes overhead. If they were, Americans would surely insist that we respond. But cyber warfare is silent warfare. I sometimes refer to it as a war without blood: there are no soldiers in the field, no bullets and bombs. But its potential to hurt is very real. Imagine, for example, a cyberattack on railroad switching signals or hospital generators or a nuclear power plant.

The intelligence community and private companies alike are waging a defensive battle against cyberattacks on a minute-by-minute basis. But we still remain unprepared for this new kind of terrain. Our systems and infrastructure need to be seriously upgraded.

We are currently under attack. Our elections are top of mind, especially given the evil—and effective—attacks by the Russian government. The January 2017 assessment found that

"Russian President Vladimir Putin ordered an influence campaign in 2016 aimed at the U.S. presidential election. Russia's goals were to undermine public faith in the U.S. democratic process, denigrate Secretary Clinton, and harm her electability and potential presidency." The intelligence community assessed, with a high degree of confidence, that Russia's intelligence services hacked into Hillary Clinton's presidential campaign to release data they gathered with the intent of influencing the outcome of the election.

Russian agents and propagandists exploited U.S. social media platforms such as Facebook, Twitter, and YouTube to spread false and scorching information about Secretary Clinton and to fuel divisions in the United States. And I think it's very telling exactly how they went about it.

They focused on hot-button issues, from race to LGBTQ and immigrant rights. This means that they knew that racism and other forms of hate have always been our nation's Achilles' heel, our weak point. They knew precisely where to strike us, deliberately targeting—and tearing away at—some of the most painful, divisive parts of our nation's history.

I first made this point during an Intelligence Committee meeting. A few days later, I was sitting at my desk on the Senate floor, the last one in the far back. I had chosen the desk for two reasons: it wasn't visible on the ever-present TV cameras, which made it easier for me to concentrate on the work at hand. But, more important, it was the desk closest to the candy drawer.

I looked up and noticed that Senator James Lankford, a Republican from Oklahoma, was walking toward me, literally crossing the aisle so we could have a conversation.

"Kamala, I've been listening to what you've been saying about race as our Achilles' heel, and I think you're on to something important," he said. "Personally, I think it starts with the question 'Have you had a family over to your house that doesn't look like you? Have you ever really had that kind of interaction?' I think that's a good place to start."

"I'm glad to hear you say that," I told him. "We have to start somewhere."

Lankford and I sat across from each other in closed sessions of the Intelligence Committee, and though there are very few things we agree about when it comes to policy, I found him to be genuinely kind and thoughtful. It didn't take long for us to build a friendship. Together with our colleagues on the committee, we studied the information that led to the January 2017 assessment about Russian attacks. Of particular interest to me was that Russians tried to break into the election infrastructures of at least eighteen individual states—things like voter registration databases. Thankfully, as of May 2018, our committee had not seen any evidence that actual vote tallies or voter registration rolls were changed. But we cannot rule out that activities were successfully carried out that we just don't know about yet.

In our report, we raised concerns about a number of potential weaknesses that remain in our election infrastructure. Voting systems are outdated, and many of them do not have a paper record of votes. Without a paper record, there is no way to reliably inspect a vote tally and confirm that numbers haven't been changed. Thirty states use paperless voting machines in some places, and five states use only paperless machines. We also found that many of our election systems are connected to the internet, leaving them open to hacking. Even systems not regularly connected to the internet are nevertheless updated by software that must be downloaded from the internet.

Cybersecurity isn't about building a wall that can never be scaled—that's not realistic. Our focus must be on defending against, detecting, preventing, managing, and limiting any effort to do us harm.

At the time, James Lankford and I were the only members of the Senate who served on both the Homeland Security and Intelligence Committees. As such, we were uniquely suited to come together in a nonpartisan way to develop legislation to combat these attacks. At the end of December 2017, together with other senators, we introduced a bill—the Secure Elections Act—that would protect the United States from future foreign interference in our elections.

However, election systems aren't the only area in which we are vulnerable to foreign meddling. In March 2018, for example, the Department of Homeland Security and the FBI issued a joint alert that showed that Russian hackers had gained access to American computer systems that control the energy we use to light our homes, the water we drink, and the airplanes that transport us from one place to another. After they got access, the Russians did extensive reconnaissance—in other words, serious snooping. They were able to gain access to at least one power plant's control system. And they snuck tools into the systems that would allow them, in certain cases, to shut down power plants at will.

This is, needless to say, a serious weakness. Millions of Americans recall the blackout of August 2003, when an electricity surge overloaded the grid covering parts of eight northeastern states. Major cities were plunged into darkness. Fire departments rushed to free people from elevators as building temperatures rose. Hundreds of trains were stopped in their tracks, and thousands of passengers had to be rescued from darkened subway tunnels. Waste treatment plants lost power; 490 million gallons of raw sewage were spilled in New York City alone. Cell phone service was disrupted. Bank money machines went down. Hospitals had to rely on generators to care for vulnerable patients. Analysts later concluded that death rates in New York City rose 28 percent during the two-day blackout.

In the intelligence community's Worldwide Threat Assessment in 2018, the director of national intelligence detailed increased risks to critical infrastructure—the big systems that pump clean water to our homes, and keep our traffic lights humming and our mobile phones charged. He said, "Russia, Iran, and North Korea . . . are testing more aggressive cyber-attacks that pose growing threats to the United States and U.S. partners."

Iran, which in the past has attacked a large U.S. corporation and stolen personal data, is expected to continue its work penetrating the United States' cyber infrastructure. North Korea, which conducted a destructive attack on Sony—the company that makes PlayStation, other electronics, and movies—in November 2014, and which the U.S. government identified as responsible for a massive cyberattack in the United Kingdom that paralyzed that country's health care system, is expected to use its cyber operations to steal money as it did in 2016, when it took $81 million from the Bangladesh Bank. China, meanwhile, has been advancing its own cyberattack capabilities since 2015 and has directed attacks at U.S. private industry, particularly manufacturers of weapons and information technology and communications firms whose products and services support worldwide networks. And this doesn't even include international criminals who hack for their own reasons.

As General Keith Alexander, former director of the National Security Agency, said in 2010, Department of Defense systems are probed by hackers about 250,000 times an hour. That's six million times each day.

In a world where tech can be weaponized, we need the very best technology in order to respond. And that means constantly upgrading our efforts so that we are always a step ahead.

It's one of the reasons I believe we must be a country that welcomes highly skilled students and professionals from around the world to study at our universities and work at our companies.

Ultimately, I believe we are going to need to develop a cyber doctrine. As a matter of principle, we will have to decide when and whether a cyberattack is an act of war, and what kind of response it warrants.

On January 12, 2017, Mike Pompeo came before the Senate Intelligence Committee for his confirmation hearing as CIA director. By tradition, questions at public hearings are asked in order of seniority, so, as the newest member of the committee, I questioned Pompeo last. Throughout the hearings, I listened as my colleagues asked Pompeo a wide range of questions, touching on traditional issues like intelligence sharing with foreign countries and preventing terrorist attacks in the United States and abroad. When it was finally my turn, I focused on a subject area that seemed to surprise Pompeo and others on the committee. I wanted to know how his public position rejecting the science of climate change was going to impact his role at the top of America's intelligence apparatus.

The CIA had already assessed that climate change was dangerous to our national security. Pompeo's previous statements ignored the CIA assessment. How would he brief the president? Would he let his personal views override the findings of CIA professionals when it came to climate change—and, if so, what would that mean for other dire threats against our nation?

Climate change can be seen from many angles. We take for granted the delicate balance that keeps our planet running, and climate change throws that balance out of whack. We'll see more floods, but also more drought. More wildfires, but also weirdly freezing winters in some places. Rising sea levels, and a sharp reduction in drinking water. Climate change threatens how we grow crops to eat, where we can build our homes and communities, and the animal and plant life all around us. Some see it purely as an environmental issue. They point to the destruction of habitats, the melting of ice sheets, and a coming mass extinction of species. Others see it as a public health issue that demands a world where clean air and clean water are easily available. There is also the economic dimension of climate change: ask farmers about their precise and measured focus on weather patterns, about the incredibly narrow temperature ranges that produce a successful harvest or a ruinous one, and you will come to understand that extreme weather events and unpredictable shifts in the climate are nothing to dismiss. These are the people who grow our food, so we ought to pay close attention.

But when you speak to military generals, when you speak to senior members of the intelligence community and experts on international conflicts, you will find that they look at climate change as a national security threat—a "threat multiplier" that will make poverty more widespread, creating conditions that heighten violence, despair, even terrorism. An unstable, unpredictable climate will cause an unstable, unpredictable world.

For example, climate change will lead to droughts. Droughts will lead to famine. Famine will drive desperate people to leave their homes in search of food. Massive flows of displaced people will lead to refugee crises, as people frantically try to get into countries where they could have a better life, or simply where food is not scarce. Refugee crises will lead to tension and instability across borders.

Climate change also increases the risk of deadly global pandemics—infectious diseases—making their way to the United States. The Centers for Disease Control and Prevention (CDC) reported that between 2006 and 2016, the number of Americans infected by diseases carried by bugs, like West Nile, Zika, and Lyme, more than tripled. As temperatures continue to warm, diseases are flourishing in parts of America where they wouldn't have been able to survive in the past. In fact, the CDC has already identified nine types of infections that had never been seen before in the United States.

The hard truth is that climate change is going to cause terrible instability and desperation, and that will put American national security at risk. That's why former CIA director John Brennan has said that when CIA analysts look for deeper causes of rising instability in the world, one of the causes they point to is climate change. That's why, as part of President Obama's national security strategy, climate change was identified as a national security threat of the highest priority. That's why the Pentagon—our Defense Department—has been developing strategies to protect the dozens of military bases around the world that will be affected by rising seas and extreme weather events. And it's why I didn't hesitate in asking the person who would become the nation's CIA director how and whether climate change would be a factor in his strategy to protect the American people.

This isn't the stuff of science fiction or of a futuristic novel. Climate-driven crisis is already on the rise. In late 2017, for example, water reserves fell so low in Cape Town, South Africa, that the city of more than three million people, South Africa's second largest, was at risk of having its taps run dry. Residents started showering over buckets so that they could reuse the water in their washing machines. Farmers had to abandon about a quarter of their crops.

This is an issue we will face at home, too, and it's a matter of national security that we prepare for it. We need to ensure a reliable, sustainable supply of clean water. Growing up in California, I understood from an early age that the water supply is precious and fragile. In elementary school, my class-mates and I studied ecology. I remember the drought of 1976 and 1977—unflushed toilets, shower timers, and dried-out brown lawns. I think a lot about water security, and I never take it for granted.

There's a lot we can learn from friends and partners who have been working on these problems for years—especially Israel, a global leader on water security issues. In February 2018, I traveled to Israel and toured its Sorek desalination plant, which produces clean drinking water from sea water. I had a glass. It tasted as good as any water I've ever had.

And that's not all. As many have said, the Israelis have made the desert bloom. They've done so in part by successfully capturing 86 percent of their wastewater—like water that goes down the drain when you brush your teeth—and purifying it for farming. By contrast, the United States, which produces 32 billion gallons of wastewater each day in cities and towns, reclaims only 7 to 8 percent. Surely we can do better than that.

Conserving water and safeguarding against scarcity must be a top priority. The same can be said, in this era of climate change, for the need to protect against floods. The destructive force of Hurricane Maria left the island of Puerto Rico in ruins. I visited Puerto Rico in November 2017 and saw some of that devastation firsthand—homes obliterated, roads collapsed and destroyed, a community in crisis, and a death toll that may be as high as 4,600 American citizens in Puerto Rico. And if it isn't floods, it's fires. Higher temperatures and longer dry spells turn our forests into kindling. California has always had wildfires, but because of climate change, they are becoming more frequent and getting bigger and bigger.

In August 2018, I flew home to California to meet with firefighters and people forced to evacuate their homes from the Mendocino Complex Fire, which burned more than 450,000 acres, making it the largest fire in the state's history.

When I arrived in Lake County, I went to a convention center where evacuated families were being sheltered temporarily. Some of them knew they had lost their homes and all of their possessions. Others were left to wonder. I met a mom who was pregnant with her third child. She was trying to keep her family's spirits up. I remember how proud her daughter was to show me how neatly she had tidied the sheets on top of the Red Cross cots where they now slept.

A year earlier, I met a firefighter who lost his own home in a fire he was fighting. He said he had always thought he understood the pain of losing everything, given how often he had seen it happen to others—but that it was so much worse than he imagined. Still, he reminded himself and me, it wasn't as bad as the families that got the call that their husband or son had been one of the many firefighters who lost their lives that year.

There is a theme that runs through all of these issues, be it cybersecurity or climate change or keeping aggressors like Russia and North Korea in check. Though the United States is a superpower, there are real limits to what we can do alone. In order to keep the American people safe, we must work in partnership with our allies, other countries that share our values and goals.

We live in an uncertain world, one filled with complexity and danger. The challenges we face in the future will require us to mobilize based on being smart, not on being afraid. There will be hard decisions to make, to be sure, of the kind that no previous generation has had to consider. And yet it will serve us well to remember what it was that helped us protect the American people and secure the peace in the generations leading up to this moment. We must remember that we are a nation of laws, that we stand for the rule of law. We must remember what we have worked and in some cases bled for:

an international order that promotes peace and cooperation; a commitment to democracy, here and around the world; a rejection of tyrants and dictators who rule their countries based on their self-interest alone, not the interests of the people they are meant to serve. Imperfect though we have been, ours is a history in pursuit of a better, safer, freer world. In the years to come, with all the challenges to come, we cannot lose sight of who we are and who we can be.

Ten

WHAT I'VE LEARNED

Early in my career, one of the first cases I tried was a car crash case in Judge Jeffrey Horner's Oakland courtroom. To illustrate my argument, I had printed out a map on a large sheet of paper, which I pinned to an easel with butterfly clips. I needed the map so that I could show the jury the driver's path.

I don't remember all the details of the case, but I do remember this map, because I kept stumbling over north, south, east, and west. I couldn't stop getting the directions wrong, so I cracked a joke before the jury making fun of my mistakes. Not long after, during a break, Judge Horner called me into his chamber. "Don't you ever do that again," he said. "You figure it out. Figure it out."

His words stuck with me, along with so many lessons I've absorbed along the way—wisdom from my mother; encouragement and guidance from family members, friends, and trusted mentors; and the powerful examples I've witnessed, both good and bad, that have shaped my understanding of how to lead, how to achieve one's goals, how we should treat one another.

While it isn't possible to reduce the complexity of these leadership lessons to simple slogans, my team and I rely on a few key phrases as touchstones and guideposts—as starting points for policy conversations and as ways to check whether we're on the right track. I'm sharing them here because they say a lot about my personal philosophy and style. And maybe they will help to shape your thinking in some way, as the wisdom earned by other people has helped shape mine.

TEST THE HYPOTHESIS

When I was a kid, I used to visit my mother in the lab, where she'd give me jobs to do. Cleaning test tubes, mainly. I think she probably knew early on that I wasn't going to follow her into the sciences. It was the humanities—like literature and history—and the arts that spoke to me, even as I was in awe of my mother and her colleagues and their work.

But when you're the daughter of a scientist, science has a way of shaping how you think. Our mother used to talk to Maya and me about the scientific method as if it were a way of life. When I'd ask her why something was the way it was, she wouldn't just give me the answer. She wanted me to form my own hypothesis, where I would come up with an idea of what the answer could be and use that as a starting point for further investigation. The key to the scientific method is to examine and challenge your assumptions. This was how she did her work in the lab. The experiments she ran each day were aimed at figuring out whether her ideas would stand after being tested. It was about kicking the tires. She would collect and analyze the data, and draw conclusions from that evidence. If the results didn't support the hypothesis, she would reevaluate.

My mother devoted her life to discovering something new, an innovation, in the fight against breast cancer. Innovation is the pursuit of what can be, unburdened by what has been. And we pursue innovation not because we're bored but because we want to make things faster, more efficient, more effective, more accurate. In science, in medicine, in technology, we embrace the culture of innovation—hypotheses, experiments, and all. We expect mistakes; we just don't want to make the same mistake twice. We expect imperfections; it's basic for us. We've gotten used to the idea that software will need to be tweaked and updated. We don't have any problem with the concept of "bug fixes" and upgrades. We know that the more we test something, the clearer we'll understand what works and what doesn't, and the better the final product or process will be.

But in the realm of public policy, of lawmaking, we seem to have trouble embracing innovation. That's in part because when you're running for public office and you stand before the voters, you aren't expected to have a hypothesis; you're expected to have "the Plan." The problem is, when you roll out any innovation, new policy, or plan for the first time, there are likely to be glitches, and because you're in the public eye, those glitches are likely to end up blaring from headlines on the front page. This can discourage policymakers from pursuing bold actions. Even so, I believe it is our obligation to do so.

The point of being a public official is to find solutions to problems, especially the most challenging, and to have a vision for the future. You have to be willing to test your hypothesis and find out if your solution works, based on facts and data. Sticking blindly to tradition should not be the measure of success.

GO TO THE SCENE

There's a small community in Southern California called Mira Loma that sits just north of the Santa Ana River, at the western edge of Riverside County. It was, for a long time, a rural community, a place of grape vineyards and dairy farms, a place where people loved to ride horses and to raise their children away from the smog of industrial Los Angeles. But in the late 1980s, things started to change.

When Americans began buying more goods from other countries, especially those in Asia, many shipping containers were ending up at Southern California harbors. So nearby huge warehouses started popping up in Riverside County into which trucks would drop off the cargo they picked up at the docks. By the time I was attorney general, there were approximately ninety such mega-complexes in Mira Loma.

Life was transformed for the 4,500 families living in Mira Loma. Farms were dug up and paved over. Traffic became unbearable. The quiet rural community was swallowed up by an industrial warehousing district. And the air turned toxic. Every day, trucks made more than 15,000 trips on Mira Loma's main roads, bringing with them soot and other pollutants. Soon Mira Loma had one of the highest rates of diesel pollution in the state.

The pollution was linked to poor lung development and other serious illnesses in Mira Loma children. The federal Environmental Protection Agency had major concerns about health dangers associated with such filthy air. But things were only getting worse.

The circumstances of Mira Loma were brought to my attention when I learned that Riverside County had approved another complex of warehouses, for another 1,500 truck trips through Mira Loma every day. Residents sued to stop it, arguing that the county had failed to take their health concerns seriously and hadn't done the work to reduce the harm this would cause to people already suffering from the foul air. They argued that the county had failed to follow state standards meant to protect communities like theirs. After reviewing the documents, I agreed.

"I want to join the lawsuit," I told my team. "Let's show those families the state has their back."

That could have been the end of it. I was confident that, with state resources behind them, the community would have what it needed to win. But taking action wasn't enough. Reading briefing documents and talking with lawyers wasn't enough. I wanted to go to the scene.

As we approached Mira Loma, I could see a towering mass of haze and smog enveloping the community and the surrounding areas. The sun shone through, but with a gray, refracted tint as the toxic cloud settled in. When I got out of the car, the pollution stung my eyes. I could taste it in the air. I could wipe the dust and soot off surfaces with my fingers.

I went into a small meeting room where members of the community had gathered to tell me their stories. One person told me that every day, when the wind changes, he starts breathing the fumes. Another told me that it's not safe for children to play outside. More than half the households had children under eighteen, and they were stuck indoors. A soft-spoken woman told me that she was glad I was there, because they had been fighting for a long time and no one ever seemed to listen.

One man told me that they have to wash the soot off their driveways, and clean their clotheslines before they hang any clothes. He worried about the trees in his backyard, which had stopped bearing fruit and were dying. And he expressed his concern for people in the community who were suffering from higher rates of cancer, asthma, and heart disease.

At first, that was all he said. But when the microphone came back to him, the group encouraged him to tell the more personal story that had brought him to the meeting.

"It's hard for me to talk about it. . . . But, I mean, I'll do it to help this community."

Through tears, he began. "I had a daughter . . . and she died before she was fifteen years old. And instead of planning for her fifteenth birthday . . . I was planning for her funeral. . . . She died of lung cancer. Sometimes it's hard for me to talk about it. But if this can help, I'm just telling my story."

It did help. The fight against the county would take place in courtrooms and conference rooms, and we would be not just the voice but the vessel through which the community's story would be told. To really understand the pain that a community is coping with, it's not enough to imagine what it must be like. Smart policies cannot be created in an isolated tower, and arguments aren't won by facts alone. What matters just as much is being there whenever possible, in person, ears and eyes wide open, talking to the people living closest to the challenge. It mattered that we were there to hear this anguished father's story and the stories of other families in Mira Loma.

EMBRACE THE MUNDANE

Bill Gates, one of the wealthiest men on the planet, is obsessed with fertilizer. "I go to meetings where it's a serious topic of conversation," he writes. "I read books about its benefits and the problems with overusing it. It's the kind of topic I have to remind myself not to talk about too much at cocktail parties, since most people don't find it as interesting as I do." Why the fascination? He explains that farmers using fertilizer produce more food crops and that 40 percent of people on earth wouldn't be alive without those higher crop outputs. It was the literal fuel for the Green Revolution, which helped lift hundreds of millions of people out of poverty. What Gates understands is that there is a big difference between announcing a plan to end world hunger and actually ending it. And closing the gap depends on seemingly ordinary details like fertilizer and weather patterns and the height of wheat.

Often in politics, the grand pronouncement takes the place of the painstaking and detail-oriented work of getting meaningful things done. This isn't to say that there's anything wrong with grand pronouncements. Good leaders excite people with a vision for the future, bold ideas that move people to action. But it is often the mastery of the fine details, the careful execution of the boring tasks, and the dedicated work done outside of the public eye that make the changes we seek possible.

My point is: you have to sweat the small stuff—because sometimes it turns out that the small stuff is actually the big stuff. I read a story once about a principal at a St. Louis elementary school who wanted to take on rampant truancy in her school. When she talked to parents, she realized that many of the kids didn't have clean clothes. Either they didn't have access to washing machines or their families couldn't afford detergent or the power had been shut off. Students were embarrassed to show up at school in dirty clothes. "I think people don't talk about not having clean clothes because it makes you want to cry or go home or run away or something," a student explained. "It doesn't feel good."

So the principal had a washer and dryer installed at her school, and she invited students who had missed more than ten days of class to do their laundry there. In the first year of the initiative, more than 90 percent of the students they tracked boosted their attendance.

WORDS MATTER

Words have the ability to empower and to trick, the power to soothe and to hurt. They can spread important ideas and wrongheaded ones. They can spur people to action, for good or ill. Words are incredibly powerful, and people in power, whose words can carry furthest and fastest, have an obligation—a duty—to speak them with precision and wisdom. Scripture tells us, "The one who has knowledge uses words with restraint, and whoever has understanding is even-tempered."

I am very aware of the potential power that lives in my words—as someone who represents nearly forty million people, who seeks to give voice to the voiceless. And so when

I speak, I do so with the knowledge that the words I choose matter.

First, what we call things, and how we define them, shapes how people think about them.

When I was attorney general, I prosecuted a case against a man who had started a horrible website called UGotPosted. com, which invited people to upload to the site sexually explicit photos and videos of people they knew. The man who ran the website would then demand payment from those who had been exploited in exchange for removing the images. It was called "revenge porn."

But I wasn't having any of that term. Revenge is something you inflict on someone who has wronged you. These victims hadn't wronged their perpetrators—quite the opposite. Bullies were preying on them. It wasn't revenge. Nor was it pornography. People who are in pornography want the public to see them. The victims here had never intended for their private images to be publicly displayed. It was internet-based extortion—threatening someone for money—plain and simple, so we referred to it as cyber exploitation. I directed my team that we were not to use the term "revenge porn." I encouraged the media not to use the term, either. And I did so for one fundamental reason: words matter.

Second, I choose to speak truth. Even when it's uncomfortable. Even when it leaves people feeling uneasy. When you speak truth, people won't always walk away feeling good—and sometimes you won't feel so great about the reaction you receive. But at least all parties will walk away knowing it was an honest conversation.

That is not to say that all truth is uncomfortable, or that the intention is to cause discomfort. Many truths are incredibly hopeful. I am simply saying that the job of an elected official is not to sing a lullaby and pretend everything is perfect. The job is to speak truth, even in a moment that does not welcome or invite its utterance.

SHOW THE MATH

In math tests in school, it usually isn't enough to simply answer a question. You have to show your work. That way, your teacher can see how your logic unfolded, step by step. If you got the solution right, the teacher would know that you hadn't just made a lucky guess. And if you got it wrong, she could see exactly where and why—and help you correct your mistake.

"Showing the math" is an approach that I've embraced throughout my career. In part, it helps me and my team test the logic of our own proposals and solutions. When we force ourselves to lay out our assumptions, we often find that there are certain parts of our arguments that assume things they shouldn't. So we go back and revisit them, we revise them, we dive deeper so that when we are ready to put forth a proposal, we can be confident in its soundness.

At the same time, I think leaders who are asking for the public's trust have a responsibility to show the math, too. We can't make other people's decisions for them, but we have to be able to show how we reached ours.

That's why, when I taught young lawyers how to put together a closing argument, I would remind them that it wasn't enough to get up in front of the jury and just tell them, "You must find eight." Their job was to get up there and show the jury that "two plus two plus two plus two" leads, unmistakably, to "eight." I'd tell them to break down every element. Explain the logic of their argument. Show the jury how they reached their conclusion.

When you show people the math, you give them the tools to decide whether they agree with the solution. And even if they don't agree with everything, they may find that they agree with you most of the way—a kind of policy-making "partial credit" that can form the basis for constructive collaboration.

NO ONE SHOULD HAVE TO FIGHT ALONE

In the spring of 1966, Cesar Chavez led a 340-mile march of Latinx and Filipino farmworkers from California's Central Valley to its state capital in an effort to draw attention to the mistreatment and terrible working conditions of his fellow farmworkers. That summer, the United Farm Workers was formed, and under Chavez's leadership, it would become one of the most important civil rights and labor rights organizations in the country.

At the same time, two thousand miles away, Dr. Martin Luther King Jr. was leading the Chicago Freedom Movement. Through speeches and rallies and marches and meetings, he demanded everything from the end of housing discrimination to high-quality education for all.

In September 1966, Dr. King sent Chavez a telegram. He wrote about the many fronts on which the battle for equality must be fought—"in the urban slums, in the sweat shops of the factories and fields. Our separate struggles are really one—a struggle for freedom, for dignity, and for humanity."

That is the sentiment I believe we must embrace. There are so many ongoing struggles in this country—against racism and sexism, against discrimination based on religion, national origin, and sexual orientation. Each of these struggles is unique.

Each deserves its own attention and effort. And it would be wrong to suggest that the differences don't matter, or that one solution or one fight will alone solve them all. But at the same time, we should embrace the point that Dr. King made to Chavez—that what these struggles have in common is the pursuit of freedom, of basic human dignity. Black Lives Matter can't just be a rallying call for black people, but a banner under which all decent people will stand. The #MeToo movement, of women standing up to abuse and harassment, cannot make lasting changes for women in the workplace unless the effort is joined by men. Victories by one group can lead to victories for others, in the courts and in society as a whole. None of us— none of us—should have to fight alone.

And if we are lucky enough to be in a position of power, if our voice and our actions can change things, don't we have a special obligation? Being an ally can't just be about nodding when someone says something we agree with—important as that is. It must also be about action. It's our job to stand up for those who are not at the table where life-altering decisions are made. Not just those people who look like us. Not just those who need what we need. Not just those who have gained an audience with us. Our duty is to improve the human condition—in every way we can, for everyone who needs it.

IF IT'S WORTH FIGHTING FOR, IT'S A FIGHT WORTH HAVING

There are nine justices on the Supreme Court. It's a lifetime job, so when a Justice retires, the president gets to choose his or her replacement, but that person needs to be confirmed by the United States Senate. The first hurdle a nominee has to pass is the Senate Judiciary Committee. I had been appointed to the Judiciary Committee ten months earlier and had expected to be part of a Supreme Court confirmation process. But when Justice Anthony Kennedy announced his retirement on June 27, 2018, I counted myself among the millions of people who were stunned and dismayed, especially when we learned that Judge Brett Kavanaugh had been chosen to replace him.

We knew from Judge Kavanaugh's public statements, his writings, and his judicial record that he was hostile to civil rights and voting rights and reproductive rights—the right of women to decide if and when to have a baby. We knew he would be a reliable vote against unions, against the environment, against regulating businesses.

We knew before his first set of confirmation hearings that there was something in his past that Judge Kavanaugh and the White House were trying to hide. We knew it because 90 percent of Judge Kavanaugh's record was withheld from members of the Judiciary Committee. We knew after those first hearings that Brett Kavanaugh had misled the Senate under oath: about his involvement with stolen documents, about his work with controversial judicial nominees, and other issues.

We knew all of this first. And then we learned something else. We learned her name. Dr. Christine Blasey Ford. And then we learned her story.

We learned that when she was in high school, Christine Blasey Ford had gone to a gathering at a house with several people, where Brett Kavanaugh had forced himself on top of her, had pushed against her, and had groped her while trying to take off her clothes. We learned that when she tried to scream, he had put his hand over her mouth, that she believed he was going to rape her, that she feared he might kill her by accident.

"I was able to get up and run out of the room," Dr. Ford explained as she testified under oath in front of the Judiciary Committee about the attack. "Directly across from the bedroom was a small bathroom. I ran inside the bathroom and locked the door. I heard Brett and [his friend] Mark leave the bedroom laughing and loudly walk down the narrow stairs, pinballing off the walls on the way down.

"I waited, and when I did not hear them come back up the stairs, I left the bathroom, ran down the stairs, through the living room, and left the house," she continued. "I remember being on the street and feeling an enormous sense of relief that I had escaped from the house and that Brett and Mark were not coming after me."

I watched her in such awe as she told her story. In front of Dr. Ford sat all twenty-one members of the Judiciary Committee, looking down from a raised dais. Behind her sat an audience of many strangers. To her left was Rachel Mitchell, an Arizona prosecutor who would question Dr. Ford instead of the Republican committee members—all men—who apparently doubted their own ability to question her. There were bodyguards in the room, too, whose protection Dr. Ford now needed. And, of course, there were the cameras, broadcasting every moment, every movement, every word spoken and tear shed in front of a national audience. This was no place for a person to have to talk about the worst day of her life.

And yet there she was in front of us and the world—even after death threats, even after having to leave her home, even after countless vile attacks hurled at her online. Christine Blasey Ford came to Washington out of a sense of what she called her civic duty and testified in one of the most extraordinary displays of courage I have seen in my lifetime. And one that would inspire others to do the same.

Judge Kavanaugh delivered his response later that day, and shortly after he finished testifying, Republican leaders scheduled a committee vote on his nomination for the following day.

The next morning, a protester named Ana Maria Archila came up to Republican senator Jeff Flake, of Arizona, in the halls of Congress. "On Monday, I stood in front of your office," she exclaimed to him as he got into an elevator. "I told the story of my sexual assault. I told it because I recognized in Dr. Ford's story that she is telling the truth. What you are doing is allowing someone who actually violated a woman to sit on the Supreme Court! This is not tolerable!"

As she spoke, Senator Flake nodded his head but didn't make eye contact. Then another survivor, Maria Gallagher, spoke up: "I was sexually assaulted and nobody believed me. I didn't tell anyone, and you're telling all women that they don't matter, that they should just stay quiet because if they tell you what happened to them you are going to ignore them. That's what happened to me, and that's what you are telling all women in America, that they don't matter."

Senator Flake continued to avoid the woman's gaze. "Look at me when I'm talking to you!" she said, her voice breaking.

"You are telling me that my assault doesn't matter, that what happened to me doesn't matter, and that you're going to let people who do these things into power. That's what you're telling me when you vote for him. Don't look away from me!" The elevators closed, and Senator Flake made his way to the room where the Judiciary Committee was holding a vote on the confirmation of Brett Kavanaugh.

There are many reasons why survivors of sexual assault don't report, and one is the fear that they will not be believed. "I was calculating daily the risk/benefit for me of coming forward, and wondering if I would just be jumping in front of a train that was going where it was going anyway," Dr. Ford had said when she testified, "and that I would just be personally annihilated."

As Republican senators pressed ahead, that fear seemed all too justified. Those senators were choosing not to believe Christine Blasey Ford, even though she had risked everything to warn them about what she knew, even though she had reached out before Judge Kavanaugh had even been nominated, even though she had no reason to lie.

They chose not to believe Dr. Ford even as they refused to do a real investigation, even though she had information that backed up her claims, even though Judge Kavanaugh had more than one accuser. For Judge Kavanaugh's defenders, the cost of believing her—the cost of the truth itself—was simply too high.

"This has been about raw power," I said after leading a walkout of the committee hearing. "You're seeing that on display in the hearing this morning; you're seeing that in the process from the beginning. . . . This is a failure of this body to do what it has always said it is about, which is to be deliberative."

When I returned to the chamber, there were rumblings. It appeared that Senator Flake had been affected by the survivors who'd stopped him in the elevator. After consultation with Senator Chris Coons, a Democrat from Delaware, and others, Senator Flake called for a delay to the final vote so the FBI could be given a week to investigate further. It was a welcome pause.

We know now that the victory felt in that moment wouldn't last—but it was still meaningful. Two survivors of sexual assault standing in front of an elevator seemed to change the mind of a senator whom most saw as immovable, securing an FBI investigation and forcing a delay in an out-of-control process. In that moment, those two brave women were more powerful than all the Democratic senators on the Judiciary Committee. Together they paused history—and gave us one last chance to prevail.

But the White House had one more card to play. The

administration limited the scope of the investigation, determining whom the FBI could speak to, even preventing agents from following up with Dr. Ford and Judge Kavanaugh themselves. And yet for key undecided senators, the fact that there had been an investigation of any kind was enough. On October 6, 2018, I stood on the Senate floor and watched as Judge Kavanaugh got confirmed.

With this lifetime appointment, Justice Kavanaugh will be in a position, along with the conservative majority on the court, to strip away a woman's right to end her pregnancy; to gut the Affordable Care Act; to kill regulations on corporations; to unravel fundamental rights to vote, to marry, and to privacy. I worry about the ways his partisanship and temperament will infect the court, how it will color his decision making, how it will disadvantage so many who seek relief in the courts. I worry about what it will do to the court itself to have a man credibly accused of sexual assault among its justices. I worry about the message that has been sent yet again to Americans and the world: that in our country, today, someone can rage, lash out, resist accountability, and still rise to a position of extraordinary power over other people's lives.

But here's what I am not worried about: I am not worried about our commitment to the fight for a better country. I am not worried that this experience has diminished our will. We chose this fight not because we were sure we could win but because we were sure it was right. Because that should be all that matters. Even though we didn't prevail, this fight mattered.

Dr. Ford did not come forward in vain. As Senator Patrick Leahy said of her decision to speak, "Bravery is contagious." The cameras and microphones that Dr. Ford never sought carried her story and her message far beyond our committee room, inspiring women and men to tell the stories of their sexual assaults, many for the first time. On the day that Dr. Ford testified, the National Sexual Assault Hotline saw a 200 percent increase in calls. Women were calling in to television stations to share their stories. Writing essays. Telling their husbands and fathers. They were speaking their truth—and, in so doing, making plainer than ever that sexual violence is more widespread than we'd like to believe.

These survivors took no pleasure in reliving their own pain. But their voices, like Dr. Ford's, will have lasting reach.

Indeed, though this battle is over, its impact is yet to be seen. History has shown that one person's willingness to stand up for what is right can be the spark that ignites far-reaching change.

I am not naive. I walk the same halls where one Republican

senator told survivors of sexual assault to "grow up," and where another described protesting survivors as a "mob," even as the president he serves was inciting a crowd to humiliate Dr. Ford. I know—we all know—that there are miles still to go before women receive the full respect and dignity we deserve. But I am heartened by the unprecedented numbers of women running for office, and the many more who have been politically energized. I am heartened by the new bonds being forged across boundaries of race, age, background, experience, and gender as women and men stand shoulder to shoulder for justice, equality, and basic rights.

This progress is the product of a movement. We will grow stronger through every effort, even when we face setbacks. We will draw wisdom from every chapter, even when those lessons are hard. We will face what is to come with conviction that change is possible—knowing that truth is like the sun. It always rises.

YOU MAY BE THE FIRST. DON'T BE THE LAST.

I was in the middle of my first campaign for district attorney when I got a call from an old law school friend, Lisa, who was working as a career counselor at a nearby law school. She had met a young black woman named Venus Johnson, a second-year law student who had grown up in Oakland, the child of an immigrant, with dreams of becoming a prosecutor back home. Not surprisingly, when my friend heard Venus's story, she thought of me.

We arranged to spend a day together in the fall of 2003, and from the moment I shook Venus's hand, I could feel this incredible sense of commonality. I could see myself in her. She was kind enough to spend the day following me around while I campaigned and ran errands. At one point, we drove past a storefront that had a sign for my opponent in the window. "Come on, let's go," I told Venus as I grabbed one of my own signs out of the trunk. We went in and I shook hands with the store owner and asked him for his support.

"But . . . um . . . I have another candidate's sign in my window," he said, not sure what to make of me.

"That's okay," I told him. "You can put mine in the window, too!" He agreed, and we were on our way.

Over lunch, Venus and I talked about the reasons she wanted to be a prosecutor, and the kind of work she had hoped to do. I learned that her father had a long career in law enforcement, and that she always imagined herself fighting on behalf of victims. I told her that I had taken a similar path and recommended she follow her instincts and go home to join the Alameda County District Attorney's Office. I'd be happy, I told her, to make some calls on her behalf.

She seemed to wonder why I was doing this for her. I told her that there was something my mother used to say that I always held close. "You may be the first. Don't be the last." My mother had gotten to where she was because of the help of mentors. I had gotten to where I was because of mentors, too. And I intended to be a mentor to as many people as I could during the course of my career.

A few years after my first conversation with Venus, she got the job she'd been dreaming of in the Alameda County DA's Office. She worked there for eight years, and, like me, she specialized in helping victims of sexual violence. We spoke regularly over those years. In 2014, she joined me in the attorney general's office, and about one year into her working for me on legislative matters, I had a specific request for her.

I called her into my office. "I want you to be my associate attorney general and my chief of staff."

There was a pregnant pause. "Me?" she asked.

"Yes, you!" I've had a lot of good fortune in my life, but I'm not sure I've ever felt as lucky as the moment she said yes. I couldn't have asked for a better member of the team.

During those years, we spent a lot of time together. We've continued to speak since our time in the attorney general's office. Sometimes about her cases. Sometimes about career moves she was considering. Once about a recipe for a really amazing chicken broth.

Venus was part of the inspiration for a speech I often give, especially in front of groups of young women. I like to induct them into what I call the "Role Models Club."

I tell them that, whatever profession they choose, they've got to keep raising their hands, to share—and take credit for—their good ideas, and to know that they deserve to rise as high as they dare to climb. I also tell them that when they see others in need, they've got to go out of their way to lift them up.

I tell them that sometimes members of the Role Models Club can feel alone. Sometimes they may think, "Do I have to carry this burden by myself?" The fact is, they will find themselves in rooms where no one else looks like them. And breaking barriers can be scary. When you break through a glass ceiling, you're going to get cut, and it's going to hurt. It is not without pain. But I ask them to look around at one another and hold that image in their brains and their hearts and their souls. I tell them to remember that they are never in those rooms alone—that we are all in there with them, cheering them on. And so when they stand up, when they speak out, when they express their thoughts and feelings, they should know that we're right there in that room with them and we've got their back. I know Venus always has mine.

I've seen a lot in my years of public service. And what I've learned can't all be boiled down. But I've come away with the firm belief that people are fundamentally good. And that, given the chance, they will usually reach out a hand to help their neighbor.

I've learned, through history and experience, that progress isn't like an escalator going up—steady and smooth. Sometimes it simply goes from one plateau to another. Sometimes we fall back tragically. Sometimes we leap forward and achieve things beyond the realm of what we thought possible. I believe that our job is to provide the force propulsion that will get us to a higher plane.

The U.S. Constitution starts with the idea that "We the People" can form a "more perfect union." We have yet to achieve that perfect union. Alongside the great achievements of the American experiment lies a dark history that we have to deal with in the present. In the face of powerful headwinds, it's easy to become tired. To become overwhelmed. But we cannot give up. The beginning of our downfall comes when we stop imagining and working for a better future. Let me speak one final truth: For all of our differences, for all the battles, for all the fights, we are still one American family, and we should act like it. We have so much more in common than what separates us. We need to paint a picture of the future in which everyone can see themselves, and everyone is seen. A vibrant portrait of a vibrant United States, where everyone is treated with equal dignity and each of us has the opportunities to make the most of our own lives. That is the vision worth fighting for, born out of love of country. It is an age-old fight. Every generation has to recommit to the work, to the effort, and to the true meaning of the word "patriot." A patriot is not someone who tolerates the conduct of our country, whatever it does; it is someone who fights every day for the ideals of the country, whatever it takes.

What I have seen, especially since becoming a United States senator, is that this is a fight born out of optimism, too. I see it in the hundreds of Dreamers walking the halls of the Capitol who believe that if they are heard, they can make a difference. And they will. I see it in the parents who traveled from all over the country to Washington with their disabled children, to show Congress the faces of those who would lose coverage if the Affordable Care Act was repealed. I see it in the women who fight every day for the right to make their own decisions about their bodies. I see it in the kids who have survived gun violence, who march and fight and organize for gun safety laws, and who have achieved significant victories that tell them a better future is possible.

When I travel the country, I see that optimism in the eyes of five- and seven- and ten-year-olds who feel a sense of purpose in being part of the fight. I see it, and feel it, in the energy of the people I meet. Yes, people are marching. Yes, people are shouting. But they are doing it from a place of optimism. That's why they've got their babies with them. That's why my parents took me in a stroller to civil rights marches. Because as overwhelming as the circumstances may be, they believe, as I do, that a better future is possible for us all.

My daily challenge to myself is to be part of the solution, to be a joyful warrior in the battle to come. My challenge to you is to join that effort. To stand up for our ideals and our values. Let's not throw up our hands when it's time to roll up our sleeves. Not now. Not tomorrow. Not ever.

Years from now, our children and our grandchildren will look up and lock eyes with us. They will ask us where we were when the stakes were so high. They will ask us what it was like. I don't want us to just tell them how we felt. I want us to tell them what we did.

ACKNOWLEDGMENTS

When I sat down to write about my life, I didn't expect the process to become a life experience of its own. During one of the most tumultuous years in recent memory, my weeks started early and ended late, and I spent most weekends working on this book: recalling the professional experiences that had led up to it; revisiting the childhood that formed my way of thinking; and reflecting on what this inflection point represents. Writing this book has reinforced for me what drew me to public service and what will always be worth fighting for, and I am so grateful to everyone in my life who helped me along the way. There are a lot of you to thank.

First, I want to thank the people of California, whom I've been so honored to represent. Thank you for believing in a brighter future for our state and our nation, and for working so hard to make it so. Thank you for believing in me, for putting your trust in me all these years. I want you to know that I try hard to earn it every day. And I want to especially thank the people who wrote letters to me and let me share excerpts in this book. Your stories matter.

I also want to thank my extraordinary Senate staff, in Washington and California, for the critical work you do each day on behalf of the American people. I am so grateful for your sense of purpose and your dedication. I know this work is personal to each of you. In particular, I want to thank Tyrone Gale, who started with me as my press secretary on day one in the Senate, and who we recently lost to cancer. Tyrone is irreplaceable. He was an exceptional talent and an exceptional person—kind, warm, generous, and deeply committed to public service. Those of us who knew him will carry his memory forward, and try each day to live up to the example he set.

Like everything in my life, this book would not have been possible without the love, support, and help of family. Doug, thank you for your advice, encouragement, and feedback on this project. Cole and Ella, you are an endless source of love and pure joy for me. As I watch you enter the world, choosing your own unique paths, it makes me so proud, every day, to be your Momala.

Maya, writing this book was like reliving our childhood.

The list of things I have to thank you for is too long for these pages. So let me use this simply to thank you for the input and insights you offered throughout this process. Thank you, also, for bringing me a brother in Tony, and for Meena. Meena, I remember you at two years old, walking around the house, literally in my shoes. Now you're a leader in your own right who has forged an important path and whose advice I cherish. Thank you for everything, especially for my baby nieces, Amara and Leela, and their amazing dad, Nik.

Thank you to my father, who, when I was a young girl, encouraged me to be fearless. Thank you to my Chittis, Sarala and Chinni, and to my uncle Balu, for the love you've shared with me across great distances. Thank you to Auntie Lenore, for being such an important part of my life, and to Uncle Aubrey, for sharing memories of those early days during the writing process. And thank you to Mimi and Denise for always encouraging me.

To Chrisette and Reggie, thank you for encouraging me to write this book at the earliest stage. I've mentioned many of my dearest personal friends in this book and could have written volumes more about the experiences we've shared. Suffice it to say, I am so grateful to Amy, Chrisette, Lo, Stacey, Vanessa, and everyone (too many to mention here) with whom I've been blessed to travel this journey of life. When people ask me the secret to life, I tell them it's having good friends who become your family. That's what you've all been for me, and what I've tried to be for you. And thank you for all the godchildren you've brought into my life.

This book would not have been possible without the support of my broader family, too—staff and former staff who have been at my side throughout the years.

Thank you to my longtime advisers, Ace Smith, Sean Clegg, and Juan Rodriguez for always being there for me, and for your insights and perspectives through the years.

I am deeply grateful to my former staff from my days as attorney general and district attorney. You've all gone off to do such wonderful things but have remained part of the family. There are so many to whom I am grateful. Special thanks to Venus Johnson, Debbie Mesloh, Brian Nelson, Lateefah Simon, Dan Suvor, Michael Troncoso, and others for all your help with this project. And thank you to Josie Duffy Rice, who is like a niece to me, for your comments and suggestions on the manuscript. I have so much respect for your perspective and your perceptions. I also want to thank John Pérez, whom I still refer to as Mr. Speaker, as well as Marc Elias for your wise counsel.

Of course, none of this would be possible without the

extraordinary team at Penguin, led by Scott Moyers. Scott, you were the best editor a person could have asked for, and I will always be grateful to you for understanding the vision of the book I wanted to write. Thank you to Jill Santopolo and her talented team at Philomel Books, in particular Ruby Shamir and Talia Benamy, for helping me share my story with younger readers. Thank you to Creative Artists Agency, in particular to Mollie Glick, David Larabell, Craig Gering, Michelle Kydd Lee, and Ryder White for all of your work to make this happen.

I want to thank my collaborators, Vinca LaFleur and Dylan Loewe, for your commitment, compassion, and yes, your patience. You made this process a joy.

And a big thank-you to their research and fact-checking team: Brian Agler, Zach Hindin, Steven Kelly, Machmud Makhmudov, Maggie Mallon, and Raul Quintana. And thank you to Dorothy Hearst for our important early work together on this project.

Finally, I want to thank all the people I love that are no longer with us. I don't know what kind of book distribution Penguin has in heaven, but Aunt Mary, Uncle Freddy, Uncle Sherman, Mr. and Mrs. Shelton, Aunt Chris, Auntie Bea, Henry Ramsey, Jim Rivaldo, Mrs. Wilson, and my grandparents: this book is a tribute to how much you meant to me, how much of my life was shaped by you, how much you mattered.

Mommy, you are the star of this book because you were the reason for everything. It's been almost ten years since we lost you, and I miss you so much. Life without you is still hard to accept. But I believe you are staring down at us. When I am stuck with a hard decision, I ask, "What would Mommy think?" And in that way, you are here. It is my sincerest hope that this book will help those who never met you understand the kind of person you were. What it meant to be Shyamala Harris. And what it means to be her daughter.

NOTES

PREFACE

xi **Shortly after, we learned:** Phil Willon, "Kamala Harris Breaks a Color Barrier with Her U.S. Senate Win," *Los Angeles Times,* November 8, 2016, http://www.latimes.com/politics/la-pol-ca-senate-race-kamala-harris-wins -20161108-story.html.

xiii **"We cannot play ostrich," he said:** Thurgood Marshall, "The Meaning of Liberty," acceptance speech after receiving the Liberty Award on July 4, 1992, http://www.naacpldf.org/press-release/thurgood-marshalls-stirring -acceptance-speech-after-receiving-prestigious-liberty-award-on-july -4-1992.

CHAPTER 1: FOR THE PEOPLE

10 **They received prominent guests:** Donna Murch, "The Campus and the Street: Race, Migration, and the Origins of the Black Panther Party in Oakland, CA," *Souls* 9, no. 4 (2007): 333–45, https://doi.org/10.1080 /10999940701703794.

35 **Unlike the District Attorney's office:** City Attorney of San Francisco, https://www.sfcityattorney.org/aboutus/theoffice.

CHAPTER 2: A VOICE FOR JUSTICE

39 **toxic waste polluted the soil:** *Pollution, Health, Environmental Racism and Injustice: A Toxic Inventory of Bayview Hunters Point, San Francisco* (San Francisco: Hunters Point Mothers Environmental Health and Justice Committee, Huntersview Tenants Association, and Greenaction for Health

& Environmental Justice, 2012), http://greenaction.org/wp-content
/uploads/2012/08/TheStateoftheEnvironment090204Final.pdf.

47   **more than nine out of ten:** Nicolas Fandos, "A Study Documents the Paucity
of Black Elected Prosecutors: Zero in Most States," *New York Times*, July 7,
2015, https://www.nytimes.com/2015/07/07/us/a-study-documents-the
-paucity-of-black-elected-prosecutors-zero-in-most-states.html.

48   **All told, we had more:** The University of London, Institute of Criminal
Policy Research, *World Prison Brief,* accessed October 25, 2018,
http://www.prisonstudies.org/highest-to-lowest
/prison-population-total?field_region_taxonomy_tid=All.

54   **Lateefah was a teenager:** Kevin Cartwright, "Activist Awarded for Work
with Troubled Youth," *The Crisis* 111, no. 1 (January/February 2004): 9,
https://books.google.com/books?id=Ice84BEC2yoC&pg.

55   **"I saw resilience in these young women":** Carolyn Jones, "Lateefah Simon:
Youth Advocate Nominated as Visionary of the Year," *SFGate*, January 5,
2015, https://www.sfgate.com/visionsf/article/Lateefah-Simon-Youth-advocate
-nominated-as-5993578.php.

56   **nearly 70 percent commit a crime:** "NRRC Facts and Trends," National
Reentry Resource Center, Council of State Governments Justice Center,
https://csgjusticecenter.org/nrrc/facts-and-trends.

59   **And it was less expensive:** U.S. Department of Justice, Office of Justice
Programs, *Back on Track: A Problem-Solving Reentry Court,* by Jacquelyn
L. Rivers and Lenore Anderson, FS 00316 (Washington, DC, September
2009), https://www.bja.gov/Publications/backontrackfs.pdf.

63   **savings many Americans have:** Board of Governors of the Federal Reserve
System, Survey of Consumer Finances, 2016 (Washington, DC, 2016),
https://www.federalreserve.gov/econres/scfindex.htm.

64   *The New York Times Magazine* **told:** Nick Pinto, "The Bail Trap," *New York
Times Magazine,* August 13, 2015, https://www.nytimes.com/2015
/08/16/magazine/the-bail-trap.html.

65   **Latino men pay nearly:** Kamala Harris and Rand Paul, "To Shrink Jails,
Let's Reform Bail," op-ed, *New York Times,* July 20, 2017, https://www
.nytimes.com/2017/07/20/opinion/kamala-harris-and-rand-paul-lets-reform
-bail.html.

67   **In the decade after we:** *33 States Reform Criminal Justice Policies Through
     Justice Reinvestment* (Philadelphia: Pew Charitable Trusts, November 2016),
     http://www.pewtrusts.org/~/media/assets/2017/08/33_states_reform
     _criminal_justice_policies_through_justice_reinvestment.pdf.

67   **And since 2010, twenty-three states:** Chris Mai and Ram Subramanian,
     The Price of Prisons: Examining State Spending Trends, 2010–2015 (New York:
     Vera Institute of Justice, May 2017), https://www.vera.org/publications
     /price-of-prisons-2015-state-spending-trends.

68   **three times more likely to:** C.K., "Black Boys Are the Least Likely of
     Any Group to Escape Poverty," *The Economist*, April 2, 2018, https://
     www.economist.com/blogs/democracyinamerica/2018/04broken-ladder.

68   **they are arrested twice as often:** C.K., "Black Boys."

68   **six times as likely as white men:** Janelle Jones, John Schmitt, and Valerie
     Wilson, *50 Years After the Kerner Commission* (Washington, DC: Economic
     Policy Institute, February 26, 2018), https://www.epi.org/publication/50
     -years-after-the-kerner-commission.

68   **sentences nearly 20 percent longer:** American Civil Liberties Union,
     "Written Submission of the American Civil Liberties Union on Racial
     Disparities in Sentencing Hearing on Reports of Racism in the Justice System
     of the United States," submitted to the Inter-American Commission on
     Human Rights, 153rd Session, October 27, 2014, https://www.aclu.org/sites
     /default/files/assets/141027_iachr_racial_disparities_aclu_submission_0.pdf.

CHAPTER 3: UNDERWATER

77   **"Garden of the Sun":** Wallace Smith, *Garden of the Sun: A History of the San
     Joaquin Valley, 1772–1939,* ed. William B. Secrest Jr., 2nd ed. (Fresno, CA:
     Craven Street Books, 2004).

78   **millions of American families:** "Many Americans Ended Up Homeless
     During the Real Estate Crisis 10 Years Ago—Here's Where They Are Now,"
     Business Insider, August 7, 2018, https://www.businessinsider.com/heres-
     where-those-who-lost-homes-during-the-us-housing-crisis-are-now-2018-8.

79   **Ten years after purchasing their home:** Alana Semuels, "The Never-Ending
     Foreclosure," *The Atlantic,* December 1, 2017, https://www.theatlantic.com
     /business/archive/2017/12/the-neverending-foreclosure/547181.

80   **There were reports of pets:** "Hidden Victims of Mortgage Crisis: Pets," NBC
     News, January 29, 2008, http://www.nbcnews.com/id/22900994/ns
     /business-real_estate/t/hidden-victims-mortgage-crisis-pets/#.W2dfby2ZOEI;
     and Linton Weeks, "The Recession and Pets: Hard Times for Snoopy," *All
     Things Considered,* NPR, April 6, 2009, https://www.npr.org/templates/story
     /story.php?storyId=102238430.

80   **Roughly 5 million homeowners:** "2010's Record-Breaking Foreclosure
     Crisis: By the Numbers," *The Week,* January 14, 2011, http://theweek.com
     /articles/488017/2010s-recordbreaking-foreclosure-crisis-by-numbers.

80   **And 2.5 million foreclosure:** "2010's Record-Breaking Foreclosure Crisis."

81   **to speed up the foreclosure process:** " 'Robo-Signers' Add to Foreclosure
     Fraud Mess," NBC News, October 13, 2010, http://www.nbcnews.com/id
     /39641329/ns/business-real_estate/t/robo-signers-add-foreclosure-fraud-mess.

84   **"a woman running for attorney general":** ProsperitasMember, "Pundits
     Explain Why Kamala Will Never Win (Oops)," YouTube video, 3:00, posted
     December 7, 2010, https://www.youtube.com/watch?v=1HemG2iLkTY.

87   **I was now ahead in the race:** Jon Brooks, "Video: Steve Cooley Prematurely
     Declares Victory Last Night," KQED News, November 3, 2010,
     https://www.kqed.org/news/4195/video-steve-cooley-prematurely-declares
     -victory-last-night.

88   **Of the nearly nine million ballots cast:** Jack Leonard, "Kamala Harris Wins
     Attorney General's Race as Steve Cooley Concedes [Updated]," *Los Angeles
     Times,* November 24, 2010, http://latimesblogs.latimes.com/lanow/2010/11
     /steve-cooley-kamala-harris-attorney-general.html.

89   **37,000 homeowners lined up:** CBS News, "The Next Housing Shock,"
     60 Minutes report, YouTube video, 14:06, posted April 3, 2011,
     https://www.youtube.com/watch?v=QwrO6jhtC5E.

92   **the lender said they could help:** California Department of Justice, "Attorney
     General Kamala D. Harris Convenes Roundtable with Foreclosure Victims,"
     YouTube video, 15:59, posted November 22, 2011, https://www.youtube
     .com/watch?v=QbycqFzva5Q.

94   **That kind of money could purchase:** "Can I Buy My Own 747 Plane—And
     How Much Would It Cost?," *The Telegraph* (UK), May 12, 2017, https:
     //www.telegraph.co.uk/travel/travel-truths/how-to-buy-an-aircraft-boeing-cost.

95 five hundred California families: "California Foreclosure Statistics: The Crisis is Not Over," April 2012, http://www.responsiblelending.org/california /ca-mortgage/research-analysis/California-Foreclosure-Stats-April-2012.pdf.

CHAPTER 4: WEDDING BELLS

107 eighteen thousand same-sex couples: "Fed Court OKs Immediate Gay Marriages in California; SF Conducts 1st," KPIX CBS San Francisco, June 28, 2013, http://sanfrancisco.cbslocal.com/2013/06/28/federal-court -oks-gay-marriage-to-resume-in-california-immediately.

110 "not because it is old": Franklin D. Roosevelt, "Address on Constitution Day, Washington, D.C.," speech delivered September 17, 1937, American Presidency Project, http://www.presidency.ucsb.edu/ws/?pid=15459.

114 hundreds of weddings that day: Malia Wollan, "California Couples Line Up to Marry After Stay on Same-Sex Marriage Is Lifted," *New York Times*, June 29, 2013, https://www.nytimes.com/2013/06/30/us/california-couples-line -up-to-marry-after-stay-on-same-sex-marriage-is-lifted.html.

119 Our first report, the results: State of California Department of Justice, Office of the Attorney General, "Report on California Elementary School Truancy Crisis: One Million Truant Students, Billions in Economic Harm," press release, September 30, 2013, https://oag.ca.gov/news/press-releases/report -california-elementary-school-truancy-crisis-one-million-truant-students.

CHAPTER 5: I SAY WE FIGHT

135 more than half of Silicon Valley's: Farhad Manjoo, "Why Silicon Valley Wouldn't Work Without Immigrants," *New York Times,* February 8, 2017, https://www.nytimes.com/2017/02/08/technology/personaltech/why-silicon -valley-wouldnt-work-without-immigrants.html.

136 She wanted to be able to tell: Phil Willon, "Newly Elected Kamala Harris Vows to Defy Trump on Immigration," *Los Angeles Times,* November 20, 2016, http://www.latimes.com/politics/la-pol-ca-senate-kamala-harris-trump -20161110-story.html.

136 nearly six million American children: Leila Schochet, "Trump's Immigration Policies Are Harming American Children," Center for American Progress, July 31, 2017, https://www.americanprogress.org/issues/early-childhood

/reports/2017/07/31/436377/trumps-immigration-policies-harming
-american-children.

143 **in the first hundred days:** Schochet, "Trump's Immigration Policies."

143 **In 2016, a quarter of all kids:** Leila Schochet, "Trump's Attack on Immigrants
Is Breaking the Backbone of America's Child Care System," Center for
American Progress, February 5, 2018, https://www.americanprogress.org
/issues/early-childhood/news/2018/02/05/445676/trumps-attack-immigrants
-breaking-backbone-americas-child-care-system.

CHAPTER 6: WE ARE BETTER THAN THIS

149 **"somehow they knew":** Sankar Raman, "A Cardiac Scientist with Heart,"
The Immigrant Story, July 10, 2017, http://theimmigrantstory.org/scientist.

150 **as much as $460 billion:** Zoe Henry, "800,000 Workers, $460 Billion in
Economic Output, Dozens of Entrepreneurs: What the U.S. Loses if DACA
Goes Away," *Inc.*, March 5, 2018, https://www.inc.com/zoe-henry/dreamer
-entrepreneurs-respond-to-daca-uncertainty.html.

154 **There's a region in Central America:** Rocio Cara Labrador and Danielle
Renwick, "Central America's Violent Northern Triangle," Council on Foreign
Relations, June 26, 2018, https://www.cfr.org/backgrounder/central-americas
-violent-northern-triangle.

154 **nearly fifty thousand people were murdered:** Labrador and Renwick,
"Violent Northern Triangle."

155 **MS-13 and the Mara 18:** Labrador and Renwick, "Violent Northern Triangle."

155 **If there was a ground zero:** Labrador and Renwick, "Violent Northern Triangle."

157 **about a 50 percent chance:** *Continued Rise in Asylum Denial Rates: Impact of
Representation and Nationality,* Transactional Records Access Clearinghouse
(TRAC) at Syracuse University, December 13, 2016, http://trac.syr.edu
/immigration/reports/448.

158 **seven hundred children had been separated:** Caitlin Dickerson, "Hundreds
of Immigrant Children Have Been Taken from Parents at U.S. Border,"
New York Times, April 20, 2018, https://www.nytimes.com/2018/04/20/us
/immigrant-children-separation-ice.html.

159 **the extraordinary stress and trauma:** Colleen Kraft, "AAP Statement Opposing
Separation of Children and Parents at the Border," American Academy of

Pediatrics, May 8, 2018, https://www.aap.org/en-us/about-the-aap/aap-press-room/Pages/StatementOpposingSeparationofChildrenandParents.aspx.

165 **"I don't know every task"**: Kamala D. Harris, U.S. Senator for California, "At Hearing on Family Separations, Harris Blasts Immoral Separations and Inhumane Detention of Pregnant Women," press release, July 31, 2018, https://www.harris.senate.gov/news/press-releases/at-hearing-on-family-separations-harris-blasts-immoral-separations-and-inhumane-detention-of-pregnant-women.

166 **resort to DNA tests**: Caitlin Dickerson, "Trump Administration in Chaotic Scramble to Reunify Migrant Families," *New York Times,* July 5, 2018, https://www.nytimes.com/2018/07/05/us/migrant-children-chaos-family-separation.html.

166 **"These mothers have given"**: "Sen. Kamala Harris Visits Otay Mesa Detention Center," NBC 7 San Diego, June 22, 2018, https://www.nbcsandiego.com/on-air/as-seen-on/Sen_-Kamala-Harris-Visits-Otay-Mesa-Detention-Center_San-Diego-486286761.html.

167 **"At night, Andriy sometimes"**: Brittny Mejia, "A 3-Year-Old Was Separated from His Father at the Border. Now His Parents Are Dealing with His Trauma," *Los Angeles Times,* July 3, 2018, http://www.latimes.com/local/lanow/la-me-ln-separation-trauma-20180627-story.html.

168 **Jefferson was stiff**: Esmeralda Bermudez, " 'I'm Here. I'm Here.' Father Reunited with Son amid Tears, Relief and Fear of What's Next," *Los Angeles Times,* July 15, 2018, http://www.latimes.com/local/california/la-me-family-reunion-20180715-htmlstory.html.

168 **a fourteen-month-old who was returned**: Lisa Desjardins, Joshua Barajas, and Daniel Bush, " 'My Son Is Not the Same': New Testimony Paints Bleak Picture of Family Separation," *PBS NewsHour,* July 5, 2018 (updated July 6, 2018), https://www.pbs.org/newshour/politics/my-son-is-not-the-same-new-testimony-paints-bleak-picture-of-family-separation.

168 **Most Americans are appalled**: Eleanor O'Neil, "Immigration Issues: Public Opinion on Family Separation, DACA, and a Border Wall," *AEIdeas* (blog), American Enterprise Institute, June 21, 2018, https://www.aei.org/publication/immigration-issues-public-opinion-on-family-separation-daca-and-a-border-wall.

CHAPTER 7: EVERY BODY

172 **$25 for example:** "2017 Employer Health Benefits Survey," Kaiser Family Foundation, September 19, 2017, https://www.kff.org/report-section /ehbs-2017-section-7-employee-cost-sharing.

172 **covered by Medicare:** "2017 Employer Health Benefits Survey."

173 **A 2016 study found:** "The Association Between Income and Life Expectancy in the United States, 2001–2014," *Journal of the American Medical Association* 315, no. 16 (2016): 1750–66, http://www.equality-of-opportunity.org/assets /documents/healthineq_summary.pdf and https://jamanetwork.com/journals /jama/article-abstract/2513561.

173 **a ten-year gap in life expectancy:** Dave A. Chokshi, "Income, Poverty, and Health Inequality," *Journal of the American Medical Association* 319, no. 13 (2018): 1312–13, https://jamanetwork.com/journals/jama/fullarticle /2677433.

174 **If they win, ten of millions:** "H.R. 1628, Obamacare Repeal Reconciliation Act of 2017," cost estimate and analysis, Congressional Budget Office, July 19, 2017, https://www.cbo.gov/publication/52939.

175 **Repealing the ACA would allow:** U.S. Department of Health and Human Services, Office of Health Policy, *Health Insurance Coverage for Americans with Pre-Existing Conditions: The Impact of the Affordable Care Act* (Washington, DC, January 5, 2017), https://aspe.hhs.gov/system/files/pdf/255396 /Pre-ExistingConditions.pdf.

177 **compared with people in other:** "How Prescription Drug Prices Compare Internationally," *Wall Street Journal,* December 1, 2015, https://graphics.wsj .com/table/GlobalDrug_1201.

177 **the same dose of Crestor:** Rachel Bluth, "Should the U.S. Make It Easier to Import Prescription Drugs?" *PBS NewsHour,* March 22, 2017, https://www .pbs.org/newshour/health/u-s-make-easier-import-prescription-drugs.

177 **Three in five Americans take:** "Public Opinion on Prescription Drugs and Their Prices," Henry J. Kaiser Family Foundation, https://www.kff.org /slideshow/public-opinion-on-prescription-drugs-and-their-prices.

177 **jacked up the price of Albuterol:** John Morgan, *A Bitter Pill: How Big Pharma Lobbies to Keep Prescription Drug Prices High* (Washington, DC: Citizens for Responsibility and Ethics in Washington, 2018), https://www

.citizensforethics.org/a-bitter-pill-how-big-pharma-lobbies-to-keep
-prescription-drug-prices-high.

180 **black Americans are more likely to die:** Robin L. Kelly, *2015 Kelly Report: Health Disparities in America* (Washington, DC: Office of Congresswoman Robin L. Kelly, IL-02, 2015), 11, https://robinkelly.house.gov/sites /robinkelly.house.gov/files/2015%20Kelly%20Report_0.pdf.

180 **In 2013, the Centers for Disease Control and Prevention:** KD Kochanek, E Arias, and RN Anderson, "How Did Cause of Death Contribute to Racial Differences in Life Expectancy in the United States in 2010?" NCHS data brief, no 125 (Hyattsville, MD: National Center for Health Statistics, July 2013), https://www.cdc.gov/nchs/data/databriefs/db125.pdf.

180 **"A baby born in Cheswolde":** Olga Khazan, "Being Black in America Can Be Hazardous to Your Health," *The Atlantic,* July/August 2018, https://www .theatlantic.com/magazine/archive/2018/07/being-black-in-america-can-be -hazardous-to-your-health/561740.

181 **Black babies are twice as likely:** Linda Villarosa, "Why America's Black Mothers and Babies Are in Life-or-Death Crisis," *New York Times Magazine*, April 11, 2018.

181 **black infants are less likely:** From the Heckler Report: "Moreover, in 1981, Blacks suffered 20 infant deaths per 1,000 live births, still twice the White level of 10.5, but similar to the White rate of 1960." U.S. Department of Health and Human Services, *Black and Minority Health,* 2; "Infant Mortality," Centers for Disease Control and Prevention, https://www.cdc.gov /reproductivehealth/maternalinfanthealth/infantmortality.htm.

181 **at least three times as likely:** Villarosa, "America's Black Mothers and Babies."

181 **A major five-year study:** New York City Department of Health and Mental Hygiene, *Severe Maternal Morbidity in New York City, 2008–2012* (New York, 2017), https://www1.nyc.gov/assets/doh/downloads/pdf/data/maternal -morbidity-report-08-12.pdf; and Nina Martin and Renee Montagne, "Black Mothers Keep Dying After Giving Birth. Shalon Irving's Story Explains Why," *All Things Considered,* NPR, December 7, 2017, https://www.npr .org/2017/12/07/568948782/Black-mothers-keep-dying-after-giving-birth -shalon-irvings-story-explains-why.

182 **"literally gets under our skin":** David Bornstein, "Treating the Lifelong

Harm of Childhood Trauma," *New York Times,* January 30, 2018, https://www.nytimes.com/2018/01/30/opinion/treating-the-lifelong-harm -of-childhood-trauma.html.

182 **have shorter lives:** Khazan, "Being Black in America."

182 **Research has even found that:** Khazan, "Being Black in America."

182 **White patients are 10 percent more likely:** Robert Pearl, "Why Health Care Is Different if You're Black, Latino or Poor," *Forbes,* March 5, 2015, https://www.forbes.com/sites/robertpearl/2015/03/05/healthcare-black -latino-poor/#650c70d37869.

182 **Black patients are also less likely:** Quinn Capers IV, "To Reduce Health-Care Disparities We Must Address Biases in Medical School Admissions," *The Hill,* April 14, 2018, https://thehill.com/opinion/healthcare/383154-to-reduce -health-care-disparities-we-must-address-biases-in-medical-school.

182–83 **more likely to get breast cancer screenings:** Pearl, "Why Health Care Is Different."

183 **regardless of their economic status:** Villarosa, "America's Black Mothers and Babies."

183 **the doctor called for:** Rob Haskell, "Serena Williams on Motherhood, Marriage, and Making Her Comeback," *Vogue,* January 10, 2018, https://www.vogue.com/article/serena-williams-vogue-cover-interview -february-2018.

183 **If someone like Serena Williams:** Haskell, "Serena Williams," *Vogue.*

184 **As of 2013, only about 9 percent:** "Diversity in the Physician Workforce: Facts & Figures 2014," Association of American Medical Colleges, 2014, http://www.aamcdiversityfactsandfigures.org.

186 **doctors in the county prescribed 1.6 million:** Melanie Saltzman, "Ohio Sues Big Pharma over Increase in Opioid-Related Deaths," *PBS NewsHour,* October 7, 2017, https://www.pbs.org/newshour/show/ohio-sues-big-pharma -increase-opioid-related-deaths.

186 **thirty-eight people died from accidental overdose:** Joel Achenbach, "No Longer 'Mayberry': A Small Ohio City Fights an Epidemic of Self-Destruction," *Washington Post,* December 29, 2016, https://www .washingtonpost.com/national/health-science/no-longer-mayberry-a-small

-ohio-city-fights-an-epidemic-of-self-destruction/2016/12/29/a95076f2
-9a01-11e6-b3c9-f662adaa0048_story.html.

186 **another forty lost their lives:** "Fentanyl and Related Drugs like Carfentanil as
Well as Cocaine Drove Increase in Overdose Deaths," in Ohio Department of
Health, *2016 Ohio Drug Overdose Data: General Findings* (Columbus, 2016),
https://www.odh.ohio.gov/-/media/ODH/ASSETS/Files/health/injury
-prevention/2016-Ohio-Drug-Overdose-Report-FINAL.pdf.

187 **"Now you can get heroin quicker":** Achenbach, "No Longer 'Mayberry.'"

187 **"One day in September":** Achenbach, "No Longer 'Mayberry.'"

187 **the violent crime rate has gone up:** Achenbach, "No Longer 'Mayberry.'"

187 **two hundred children were placed:** Paula Seligson and Tim Reid,
"Unbudgeted: How the Opioid Crisis Is Blowing a Hole in Small-Town
America's Finances," Reuters, September 27, 2017, https://www.reuters.com
/article/us-usa-opioids-budgets/unbudgeted-how-the-opioid-crisis-is
-blowing-a-hole-in-small-town-americas-finances-idUSKCN1BU2LP.

188 **259 million prescriptions for opioids:** Julia Lurie, "A Brief, Blood-Boiling
History of the Opioid Epidemic," *Mother Jones*, January/February 2017,
https://www.motherjones.com/crime-justice/2017/12/a-brief-blood
-boiling-history-of-the-opioid-epidemic.

188 **roughly 80 percent of Americans:** Keith Humphries, "How Legal Drug
Companies Helped Revive the Heroin Trade," *Wonkblog, Washington Post,*
June 15, 2018, https://www.washingtonpost.com/news/wonk/wp/2018
/06/15/how-legal-drug-companies-helped-revive-the-heroin-trade.

189 **a quarter of what it would cost:** Emmie Martin, "The Median Home Price in
the U.S. Is $200,000—Here's What That Will Get You Across the Country,"
CNBC, June 29, 2017, https://www.cnbc.com/2017/06/29/what-the-medi-
an-home-price-of-200000-will-get-you-across-the-us.html.

189 **it doesn't even pay:** Farran Powell, "What You Need to Know About College
Tuition Costs," *U.S. News & World Report*, September 19, 2018, https://
www.usnews.com/education/best-colleges/paying-for-college/articles/
what-you-need-to-know-about-college-tuition-costs.

CHAPTER 8: THE COST OF LIVING

196 **"Most of the tubs":** Steven Ross, Allison Graham, and David Appleby, *At the River I Stand* (San Francisco: California Newsreel, 1993), documentary film, 56 min., https://search.alexanderstreet.com/preview/work/bibliographic _entity%7Cvideo_work%7C1858429.

197 **"So often we overlook":** Martin Luther King Jr., "All Labor Has Dignity," King Series, ed. Michael K. Honey (Boston: Beacon Press, 2011).

198 **"We are tired," Dr. King said:** King, "All Labor Has Dignity."

202 **a year of child care for a baby:** Tanza Loudenback, "In 33 US States It Costs More to Send Your Kid to Childcare Than College," *Business Insider,* October 12, 2016, http://www.businessinsider.com/costs-of-childcare-in-33 -us-states-is-higher-than-college-tuition-2016-10.

202 **more than three times faster:** Michelle Jamrisko and Ilan Kolet, "College Costs Surge 500% in U.S. Since 1985: Chart of the Day," Bloomberg, August 26, 2013, https://www.bloomberg.com/news/articles/2013-08-26/college -costs-surge-500-in-u-s-since-1985-chart-of-the-day.

204 **less than 1 percent of the homes:** Jenny Luna, "Buying a Home Is Nearly Impossible for Teachers in These Cities," *Mother Jones,* February 4, 2017, https://www.motherjones.com/politics/2017/02/buying-house-nearly -impossible-teachers-these-cities-2.

205 **more than $21,000 behind:** Brandie Temple and Jasmine Tucker, *Equal Pay for Black Women* (Washington, DC: National Women's Law Center, July 2017), https://nwlc.org/resources/equal-pay-for-black-women.

206 **worker wages grew 90 percent:** Lawrence Mishel, Elise Gould, and Josh Bivens, *Wage Stagnation in Nine Charts* (Washington, DC: Economic Policy Institute, 2015), http://www.epi.org/publication/charting-wage-stagnation.

207 **workers' pay rose just 9 percent:** Mishel, Gould, and Bivens, *Wage Stagnation.*

207 **CEOs making more than three hundred:** Diana Hembree, "CEO Pay Skyrockets to 361 Times That of the Average Worker," *Forbes,* May 22, 2018, https://www.forbes.com/sites/dianahembree/2018/05/22/ceo-pay -skyrockets-to-361-times-that-of-the-average-worker.

208 **43 percent of households can't afford:** Quentin Fottrell, "50 Million American Households Can't Even Afford Basic Living Expenses,"

MarketWatch, June 9, 2018, https://www.marketwatch.com/story/50-million
-american-households-cant-afford-basic-living-expenses-2018-05-18.

209 **2.5 million jobs in a range of industries:** Karen Harris, Austin Kimson, and
Andrew Schwedel, "Quick and Painful: Brace for Job Automation's Next
Wave," Bain and Company, March 7, 2018, http://www.bain.com/publications
/articles/quick-and-painful-brace-for-job-automations-next-wave-labor-2030
-snap-chart.aspx.

210 **In 2017, extreme weather events:** Jeff Goodell, "Welcome to the Age
of Climate Migration," *Rolling Stone,* February 25, 2018, https://www
.rollingstone.com/politics/politics-news/welcome-to-the-age-of-climate
-migration-202221.

CHAPTER 9: SMART ON SECURITY

220 **490 million gallons:** Andrea Elliott, "Sewage Spill During the Blackout
Exposed a Lingering City Problem," *New York Times,* August 28, 2003,
https://www.nytimes.com/2003/08/28/nyregion/sewage-spill-during-the
-blackout-exposed-a-lingering-city-problem.html.

220 **death rates in New York City:** G. Brooke Anderson and Michelle L. Bell,
"Lights Out: Impact of the August 2003 Power Outage on Mortality in New
York, NY," *Epidemiology* 23, no. 2 (March 2012): 189–93, https://www.ncbi
.nlm.nih.gov/pmc/articles/PMC3276729.

221 **six million times each day:** Keith Alexander, "U.S. Cybersecurity Policy and
the Role of USCYBERCOM," transcript of remarks at Center for Strategic
and International Studies Cybersecurity Policy Debate Series, Washington,
DC, June 3, 2010, https://www.nsa.gov/news-features/speeches-testimonies
/speeches/100603-alenander-transcript.shtml.

224 **diseases are flourishing:** Centers for Disease Control and Prevention,
"Illnesses from Mosquito, Tick, and Flea Bites Increasing in the US," press
release, May 1, 2018, https://www.cdc.gov/media/releases/2018/p0501-vs
-vector-borne.html.

224 **the CDC has already identified:** Centers for Disease Control and Prevention,
"Mosquito, Tick, and Flea Bites."

225 **Farmers had to abandon:** Krista Mahr, "How Cape Town Was Saved from

Running Out of Water," *Guardian,* May 4, 2018, https://www.theguardian
.com/world/2018/may/04/back-from-the-brink-how-cape-town-cracked
-its-water-crisis.

226 **reclaims only 7 to 8 percent:** U.S. Environmental Protection Agency and
CDM Smith, *2017 Potable Reuse Compendium (Washington, DC, 2017),
30,* https://www.epa.gov/sites/production/files/2018-01/documents
/potablereusecompendium_3.pdf.

227 **as high as 4,600 American citizens:** See Nishant Kishore et al., "Mortality in
Puerto Rico After Hurricane Maria," *New England Journal of Medicine*
379, no. 2 (July 12, 2018): 162–70, https://www.nejm.org/doi/full/10.1056
/NEJMsa1803972#article_citing_articles.

CHAPTER 10: WHAT I'VE LEARNED

238 **helped lift hundreds of millions:** Bill Gates, "Here's My Plan to Improve Our
World—and How You Can Help," *Wired,* November 12, 2013, https://www
.wired.com/2013/11/bill-gates-wired-essay.

239 **"I think people don't talk":** Mimi Kirk, "One Answer to School Attendance:
Washing Machines," *CityLab,* August 22, 2016, https://www.citylab.com
/solutions/2016/08/school-attendance-washing-machines/496649.

246 **Kavanaugh had misled the Senate:** Paul Blumenthal and Jennifer Bendery,
"All the Lies Brett Kavanaugh Told," *Huffington Post,* October 1, 2018,
https://www.huffingtonpost.com/entry/brett-kavanaugh-lies_us
_5bb26190e4b027da00d61fcd.

246 **We learned that when she was in high school:** "Kavanaugh Hearing:
Transcript," *Washington Post* (transcript courtesy of Bloomberg Government),
https://www.washingtonpost.com/news/national/wp/2018/09/27/kavanaugh
-hearing-transcript. Subsequent references to information presented during
the Kavanaugh hearing may also be found here.

248 **"This is not tolerable!":** Niraj Chokshi and Astead W. Herndon, "Jeff Flake
Is Confronted on Video by Sexual Assault Survivors," *New York Times,*
September 28, 2018, https://www.nytimes.com/2018/09/28/us/politics
/jeff-flake-protesters-kavanaugh.html.

248 **"that they don't matter":** Jesus Rodriguez, "Woman Who Confronted Flake
'Relieved' He Called for Delaying Kavanaugh Vote," *Politico,* September 28,

2018, https://www.politico.com/story/2018/09/28/jeff-flake-protester
-kavanaugh-852971.

249 **"I was calculating daily the risk/benefit":** "Kavanaugh Hearing: Transcript."

252 **a 200 percent increase in calls:** Holly Yan, "The National Sexual Assault
Hotline Got a 201% Increase in Calls During the Kavanaugh Hearing,"
CNN, September 28, 2018, https://www.cnn.com/2018/09/24/health
/national-sexual-assault-hotline-spike/index.html.

INDEX